D0956136

EMBRACING COMPASSION

Embracing Compassion

A Revolution in Leadership

Daisaku Ikeda

SELECTED ADDRESSES
VOLUME 2: 2004–2005

World Tribune
Press

Published by World Tribune Press
606 Wilshire Blvd.
Santa Monica, CA 90401

© 2009 Soka Gakkai

ISBN 978-1-932911-83-1

Cover and interior design by Gopa and Ted2, Inc.

10 9 8 7 6 5 4 3 2 1

Contents

Editor's Note   vii

2004

1: Affirming the Importance of the Path of Mentor
   and Disciple   1

2: Fostering Individuals of Genuine Commitment   11

3: Fostering the Children, the Successors of *Kosen-rufu*   19

4: The Lifeblood of Faith Lies in the Practice of *Shakubuku*   29

5: Live With Eternity, Happiness, True Self and Purity   37

6: Shine the Most Brilliantly Where You Are   43

7: Don't Waste a Single Day   51

8: Advancing With the Same Mind as Nichiren Daishonin   61

2005

9: Initiate a Leadership Revolution   71

10: Promoting a Culture of Peace   79

11: None Are More Noble Than Those Who Strive
   Wholeheartedly for *Kosen-rufu* 85

12: Seek Out Training That Will Make Your Life Shine 93

13: Faith Is the Ultimate Courage 101

14: Each Person Has a Unique Mission 107

15: Live With Passion, Live Without Regrets 115

Index (volumes 1 and 2) 123

Ediitor's Note

"The mission of a leader is to put everyone's mind at ease," SGI President Daisaku Ikeda tells us on page 8 of *Embracing Compassion*, vol. 1. "Toward that end, it is very important to offer words and take actions that abound with compassion."

In August 2001, the first Soka Gakkai Nationwide Executive Conference met in Karuizawa. This conference has been held every summer since then. *Embracing Compassion*, volume 1, brings together President Ikeda's speeches at those gatherings from 2001 through 2003, while volume 2 comprises speeches from 2004 and 2005.

Although his words are directed to those who have taken responsibility in the Soka Gakkai International to care for each individual member, they offer significant lessons for us all.

The following abbreviations appear in some citations:

- GZ, page number(s)—refers to *Nichiren Daishonin gosho zen-shu* (The Collected Writings of Nichiren Daishonin), the Japanese-language compilation of Nichiren Daishonin's writings (Tokyo: Soka Gakkai, 1952)
- LS(chapter number), page number(s)—refers to *The Lotus Sutra*, translated by Burton Watson (New York: Columbia University Press, 1993)

- OTT, page number(s)—refers to *The Record of the Orally Transmitted Teachings*, the compilation of Nichiren's oral teachings on the Lotus Sutra; translated by Burton Watson (Tokyo: Soka Gakkai, 2004)
- WND-1 and WND-2—refer to *The Writings of Nichiren Daishonin*, volumes 1 and 2 respectively (Tokyo: Soka Gakkai, 1999 [vol. 1] and 2006 [vol. 2])

Affirming the Importance of the Path of Mentor and Disciple

JULY 26, 2004

Thank you all for traveling such a long way for this annual Nationwide Executive Conference.

Through everyone's valiant endeavors during the first half of this year, the Soka Gakkai scored a truly momentous achievement that will go down in the annals of *kosen-rufu*. This is entirely due to the sincere, steadfast and persevering efforts of all our noble members throughout Japan. I would like to express my deepest gratitude to everyone.

Today, let's have a meaningful and productive discussion about our direction and upcoming activities for the rest of 2004. Let's make it a meeting where we all become more refreshed and invigorated mentally and physically as we proceed.

The Kosen-rufu *Movement Permits No Stagnation*

Former Chinese Premier Zhou Enlai, for whom I have the deepest respect and admiration, dedicated his entire life to fighting for the revolutionary ideals he championed as a youth. After completing one struggle, he moved forward to the next, advancing from victory to victory. He spent his life dashing from today to tomorrow, from this year to the next. This is the mark of a true revolutionary. The Soka Gakkai is an organization committed to the realization of *kosen-rufu*. The *kosen-rufu* movement permits no stagnation. We need to continuously advance and grow—this is the way of life of those who uphold the Mystic Law, a source of limitless vitality that is never deadlocked.

The Indispensable Role of Mentors

Swami Vivekananda was a respected thinker of early modern India. In February 2004, I received an honorary doctorate of literature from Rabindra Bharati University of Kolkata [Calcutta] in West Bengal State, an institution of higher learning with deep links to the great Indian writer, poet and thinker Rabindranath Tagore. The university's vice chancellor, Dr. Bharati Mukherjee, who traveled to Japan especially for the occasion and with whom I engaged in a friendly discussion, is known for her research on the thoughts of Vivekananda.

The French author Romain Rolland wrote a biography of Vivekananda. In it, the Indian spiritual leader refers to his mentor, the thinker Sri Ramakrishnan, and declares that all that he is comes from that single source, his mentor, and that he has not even one infinitesimal thought of his own to unfold.[1] In every realm of human activity, people are fostered by the relationship with their mentors, their teachers.

Nichiren Daishonin asserted, "If teacher and disciple are of different minds, they will never accomplish anything" (WND-1, 909).

My mentor was second Soka Gakkai president Josei Toda. He was a great yet strict teacher. He was always grilling me about what I had been studying. "Daisaku, what are you reading now?" he would ask. "Tell me what it's about."

At the same time, he trusted me completely and was very kind to me. If I was out of his sight for even a few moments, he would ask, "Where's Daisaku?" He wanted me at his side at all times. We were together from morning to night, allowing him to devote all his energy to fostering me.

When I was arrested on trumped-up charges during the Osaka Incident, President Toda was prepared to take my place in jail.

[On July 3, 1957, SGI President Ikeda, then Soka Gakkai youth division chief of staff, was arrested on charges of violating the election law. The accusations were groundless, and after two weeks of detention and interrogation, he was released on July 17.]

While I was in detention, President Toda dragged his frail body to the Osaka District Prosecutor's office to demand my release. "How long do you intend to keep my innocent disciple locked up?" he roared at the chief public prosecutor. "If it is me you want, arrest me now!" His spirited remonstrance overflowed with his love for his disciple. I am so grateful to have had such a mentor.

Oneness of Mentor and Disciple Is the Key

The mentor-disciple relationship is the heart of Buddhism; it is the key to limitless growth and self-improvement and the path to the unending triumph of truth and justice. I was physically weak when I was young, and the doctors said I probably wouldn't live beyond age thirty. I felt that my time was limited, and I wanted to spend my youth without regrets. That's why I advanced single-mindedly on the path of mentor and disciple. I sincerely and trustingly followed my mentor's instructions.

I acted solely in accord with the Buddha's intent. I never entertained an ambition to become this or that or to receive any special kind of treatment. All I wanted to do was to protect Mr. Toda and devote my life to his service. That was my prayer. I would be satisfied if I could set an example for future generations of how a true disciple of Mr. Toda, a mentor without parallel, should lead his or her life.

My mentor poured his heart and soul into fostering me, and I responded in kind by replying to his expectations with the whole of my being. I am what I am today because of that struggle of mentor and disciple, transcending life and death.

Likewise, the Soka Gakkai has achieved its present global development because we have dedicated ourselves to propagating the Law in the spirit of the oneness of mentor and disciple taught by Nichiren Daishonin. This is a fact that we cannot ever afford to forget or ignore. I affirm it here today for the sake of posterity.

Valuing the Opinions of Women

The youth division members are truly to be commended for their achievements. The efforts of the young women's division members have been particularly noteworthy.

Our young women of *kosen-rufu* are working energetically for the happiness of their friends, for Buddhism and for society. Nothing could be more admirable or beautiful. The foundations for everlasting happiness in life are built in the course of carrying out SGI activities. I offer sincere prayers each day for the health, happiness and safety of the young women's division members. The women's division members are also to be commended for their tremendous efforts. The age of the women of Soka has arrived.

Especially here in Japan, I hope that our male leaders will always listen to the opinions of women and take utmost heed of what they have to say, so that our women's and young women's division members can participate in activities in the most rewarding and meaningful manner possible. Leaders must not be arrogant. Arrogance points to a lack of genuine leadership ability; such people use their authority or position to order others around. It is vital that leaders respond promptly and effectively to the requests of the women's and young women's division members. Such sincere actions will speed up the advancement of *kosen-rufu* exponentially.

In any event, I particularly wish to stress the importance of men showing the utmost respect and courtesy toward the women's and young women's division members, who are striving so earnestly for *kosen-rufu*. Let's all promise to do so right here and now.

Winning through the Unity of "Many in Body, One in Mind"

The ancient Greek philosopher Aristotle said, "The man who is to be happy will therefore need virtuous friends."[2] Wonderful friendships and relationships with people of all ages enrich our lives.

It is our tradition in the Soka Gakkai for seniors to raise their juniors to become even more capable than themselves. It is deplorable for seniors to be envious of their juniors' growth or to sit back and take credit for their juniors' hard work. When seniors pray sincerely for the development of their juniors and do whatever they can for them, their generosity of spirit and bigheartedness will inspire and encourage their juniors. Their juniors in turn will want to live up to their expectations and exert themselves harder to grow and improve. This will give rise to mutual trust and unity between both parties.

Nichiren Daishonin wrote:

> [My followers] should chant Nam-myoho-renge-kyo with the spirit of many in body but one in mind, transcending all differences among themselves to become as inseparable

as fish and the water in which they swim. This spiritual bond is the basis for the universal transmission of the ultimate Law of life and death. Herein lies the true goal of Nichiren's propagation. (WND-1, 217)

The Gakkai has triumphed through the faith of its members who are united in the spirit of "many in body, one in mind"; it has triumphed through the unity of faith.

Let's further solidify our unity in the remaining months of the year and advance as one in heart and mind toward the goal entrusted to us by Nichiren, the widespread propagation of the Mystic Law throughout the world.

The Soka Gakkai Spirit

I'd like to share words of wisdom of some of the world's great thinkers with you.

The renowned German writer Johann Wolfgang von Goethe said, "I must deal firmly with anyone who attempts to obstruct my actions for good."[3] *Kosen-rufu*, the endeavor to realize peace, the highest good of all, is a struggle. Fighting resolutely against anyone who would obstruct our actions for good—this fighting spirit is the true Gakkai spirit.

"Full of foes is the world," the German poet Friedrich von Schiller wrote. "On every path, deceit / Has set its insidious traps / To ensnare pure-hearted innocence."[4]

"Insidious traps"—this is indeed an apt description of today's world. That is why those who champion good must triumph. That is why they must unite.

On the tomb of Wang Anshi, a renowned statesman and poet of China's Northern Song dynasty, are the words, "Though one may possess righteousness, one must fight if one wishes to eliminate evil."[5] How true this is.

The American philosopher Ralph Waldo Emerson observed perceptively, "The immense power of rectitude is apt to be forgotten in politics."[6] The political authorities seek to exploit the labor and strength of the people for their own ends, but the people must not let themselves be fooled! The people need to unite together and assert the "power of rectitude." This was Emerson's call.

Protecting This Realm of Beautiful Harmony

By waging its struggles based on the spirit of mentor and disciple, the Soka Gakkai has won over all obstacles. We must never allow anyone to destroy this fundamental spirit. The most treacherous villains appear from within. This is an unchanging pattern found even in the time of Shakyamuni and Nichiren.

Kautilya, a brilliant prime minister of ancient India, declared: "For the king, there is [danger of] revolt in the interior or in the outer regions. Because of danger as from a snake, a rising in the interior is a greater evil than a rising in the outer regions. . . ."[7]

The ancient Greek dramatist Sophocles composed these evocative words for one of his plays:

> I would as lief [soon] a man should cast away
> The thing he counts most precious, his own life,
> As spurn a true friend. . . .[8]

To betray one's mentor is to betray oneself. The negative causes made by those erstwhile members who scorned the Gakkai and betrayed their fellow members are certain to manifest clearly in their own lives.

Aristotle taught the importance of seeing through pretention and hypocrisy, "Falsehood is in itself mean and culpable, and truth noble and worthy of praise."[9]

Let's fight! Faith is a struggle. Life is a struggle. It is through struggle that we become strong and find our way to happiness.

The important thing is that we create something of value and that we create unforgettable memories.

The Chinese author Lu Xun wrote, "Without external stimulus, we lose the spirit of self-improvement."[10]

I especially hope that young people will rise up to shoulder full responsibility for *kosen-rufu* and open a new path to the future.

It is my dearest wish that all of our members, without exception, will lead wonderful lives crowned with brilliance to the very end.

I hope all of you, our top leaders, will set an example with your brightly burning fighting spirit as we embark on the final few months of this year and continue to strive together to construct a firm and unshakable foundation for our movement in the twenty-first century.

From the July 30, 2004, Seikyo Shimbun

NOTES

1 Romain Rolland, *The Life of Vivekananda and the Universal Gospel,* translated by E. F. Malcolm-Smith (Calcutta: Advaita Ashrama, 1975), p. 91.

2 Aristotle, "Nicomachean Ethics" (Bk. IX: Ch. 9), in *Introduction to Aristotle,* edited by Richard McKeon (New York: The Modern Library, 1947), p. 514.

3 Translated from Japanese. Johann Wolfgang von Goethe, *Shinjitsu ni ikiru—Gete no kotoba II* (Dedicated to Truth—Quotes by Goethe II), compiled and translated by Taisuke Seki (Tokyo: Shakai Shiso-sha, 1970), p. 191.

4 Translated from German. Friedrich Schiller, *Die Braut von Messina, oder Die Feindlichen Brüder* (Stuttgart: Philipp Reclam Jun., 1969), pp. 46–47.

5 Translated from Japanese. Shunpei Niwa, *So meishin genko roku* (Chronicles of the Words and Deeds of Famous Song Dynasty Ministers), in *Chugoku koten*

hyakugen hyakuwa (Quotes from the Chinese Classics) (Tokyo: PHP Kenkyusho, 1988), vol. 12, p. 190.

6 Ralph Waldo Emerson, *The Later Lectures of Ralph Waldo Emerson: 1843–71*, edited by Ronald A. Bosco and Joel Myerson (Athens, Georgia: The University of Georgia Press, 2001), vol. 1 (1843–54), p. 275. "Address to the Citizens of Concord on the Fugitive Slave Law," May 3, 1851.

7 *The Kautiliya Arthasastra, Part II,* translated by R. P. Kangle (Bombay: University of Bombay, 1972), p. 390.

8 *Sophocles: Oedipus the King, Oedipus at Colonus, and Antigone,* translated by F. Storr (Cambridge, MA: Harvard University Press, 1962), vol. 1, p. 57.

9 Aristotle,"Nicomachean Ethics" (Bk. IV: Ch. 7), in *Introduction to Aristotle,* edited by Richard McKeon (New York: The Modern Library, 1947), p. 393.

10 Translated from Japanese. Lu Xun, *Ro Jin senshu* (Selected Writings of Lu Xun), translated by Shigeo Matsueda (Tokyo: Iwanami Shoten, 1986), vol. 5, p. 9.

Fostering Individuals
of Genuine Commitment

JULY 27, 2004

Enabling all people to realize genuine happiness—that was the sole wish of my mentor, Josei Toda. He didn't care about gaining social status, celebrity or personal wealth. What mattered to him was the welfare of each individual, each member. He was willing to fight at the risk of his own life to realize this goal. He refused to condone wrongs that caused people suffering, and he spoke out resolutely for truth and justice. This passionate commitment to fight for what is right is the true Soka Spirit of mentor and disciple.

Everything I am comes from my mentor, Josei Toda. His ideas, his philosophy are the foundation of my being. Today, I would like to share some of his guidance with you.

First of all, there are these strict words he directed to Soka Gakkai leaders:

"Safeguard the Gakkai's future; never retreat a single step!"

"What are the qualities needed for good leaders? Strength and capability."

"The Gakkai spirit means making dedicated efforts for *kosen-rufu*."

Evaluating leaders on actual accomplishment or real ability is the Gakkai tradition. How successful has a person been at introducing others to Buddhism? At broadening the network of understanding for our movement? At fostering members? At protecting the Gakkai? It is important to apply such concrete criteria in evaluating leaders and their performance, praising those who are doing well on the one hand, while taking steps to deal appropriately with those who are not. "The Gakkai must always base personnel decisions on whether a person is truly capable in terms of faith and practice"—that was Mr. Toda's strict instruction.

Attaining an Environment Where Peace and Security Reign

Mr. Toda said with great severity: "Expelling liars and arrogant people from the harmonious ranks of the Gakkai will hasten *kosen-rufu* and enable us to achieve true unity and solidarity. Only then will we have a realm where everyone can advance with complete satisfaction and happiness." Soka Gakkai leaders must never forget this vigorous spirit to protect the purity of our realm of faith.

Mr. Toda also encouraged members of the youth division working hard behind the scenes, "By earnestly challenging yourself amid a difficult situation, you can attain true greatness as a human being." His guidance always overflowed with deep compassion and understanding.

In the period immediately after World War II, the Japanese economy and society as a whole were in a state of disarray that cannot possibly be imagined today. Yet President Toda declared forcefully: "We mustn't allow ourselves to be swayed by the ups and downs of the times. We will never be able to accomplish the great task of *kosen-rufu* if we are so weak and fainthearted."

No matter how trying our circumstances may be, we who embrace the Gohonzon can attain a state of life that enables us to enjoy an environment where peace and security reign—mirroring the words of the Lotus Sutra, "This, my land, remains safe and tranquil" (LS16, 230). That is the purpose of Buddhism, the purpose of our faith.

The Key to Development

Next, let me share guidance that Mr. Toda gave to the young women's division, "The Soka Gakkai's strength lies in the fact that it is based on a sound philosophy."

When Mr. Toda was further asked about the key to the organization's development, he replied simply, "Fostering youth." The growth of our young people will decide the course of our organization and the degree to which it can develop. That is why Mr. Toda was quite strict with young people. On various occasions, he said to us:

"Young people must shoulder the full responsibility for building an ideal Soka Gakkai. I am counting on you for that."

"People are of the essence. Everything depends on people. Everything depends on each individual."

"The great undertaking of *kosen-rufu* is a struggle against devilish functions. We cannot afford to cower at their onslaughts. If we allow them to defeat us, humanity will be forever enveloped in darkness."

As the lives of Nichiren Daishonin, President Makiguchi and President Toda demonstrate, a life dedicated to *kosen-rufu* is one of never-ending struggle against devilish functions. Buddhism entails a constant battle against these relentless foes. If we fail to fight these negative forces, we are "betraying the Buddha's teaching" (WND-1, 286).

It is the mission of youth to inherit this fighting spirit.

Putting the Welfare of the People First

Now let me share some of President Toda's remarks about government: "Politicians today have no guiding ideals. They are not leaders, and we are in dire need of good leaders." Government exists for the welfare of the people—that was Mr. Toda's unwavering belief.

He also said, "Political leaders need to possess strong vitality, but that vitality must be based on their concern for the nation and a commitment to truth and justice." And he noted: "If political leaders take a casual, lackadaisical approach to the task of governing, the people will suffer. Such an approach is equally detrimental in business enterprises and other organizations."

Nichiren Daishonin declared that the people are parent and sovereign, while those who govern are there to serve the people.

[Nichiren wrote, "A king sees his people as his parents" (WND-2, 809). He also rebuked Hei no Saemon, a powerful figure in the Kamakura military government, saying, "You act as hands and feet for the multitude of people" (WND-2, 318).]

When these positions are reversed and the people, who should be sovereign, are regarded as the tools of the ruling authorities, government becomes hopelessly corrupt. That is why Mr. Toda called on us to "keep a close watch on politics and government."

Mr. Toda profoundly lamented the existence of corruption and crookedness in politics: "Far too many politicians pretend to be concerned about the welfare and happiness of the people, while actually only making use of their positions to accumulate wealth and prosperity for themselves." He also said, "It is wrong to abuse one's position as an elected representative and cause trouble to many people."

Mr. Toda hoped for the appearance of political leaders who

possessed "a grand, hundred-year vision" for the nation's future. He also had strict advice for Gakkai members who wished to enter politics: "I hope that you will live your lives with the people, fight for them and die among them. People in our world today are thirsting for true political leaders who are free of self-interest."

Mr. Toda was very strict with those in positions of responsibility, and he could keenly discern their real natures. "In a crunch, the true colors of those who are cowards, self-seekers, hypocrites and pretenders are revealed." We have all seen people who talk big but accomplish nothing. Worse, in their hearts, they are contemptuous of those who are sincere and earnest. In a crisis, these are the types who betray their comrades. Don't trust such dishonorable people, and don't let them get away with such behavior—that was Mr. Toda's stern warning.

Caring Based on Faith

No one is as noble and admirable as those working for *kosen-rufu*. Mr. Toda said to Soka Gakkai leaders, "You should love the members of your local organizations as if they were your own children and care for them with dignity, care for them with faith." This is an extremely important point.

Our care should always be grounded not in a mundane, secular approach but in faith, with us chanting and taking action together with our members.

The World's Supreme Philosophy

To the young women's division, Mr. Toda called out, "The Soka Gakkai brings happiness to the people of the world through the philosophy of religion—in other words, through the world's supreme philosophy." The highest philosophy of religion is found through studying Nichiren Buddhism, the writings of Nichiren Daishonin.

As members of the young women's division, you possess the world's supreme and most wonderful philosophy, and you have a mission to share it with your friends. I hope you will proudly continue to expand your youthful network of happiness.

Mentor and Disciple Are One

What is the power of youth? It lies not in authority, titles or appearances. Mr. Toda said: "Ability is what matters for youth. It is crucial to make an earnest effort to forge yourself, to throw yourself earnestly into cultivating the strength to win over all."

That is why I fought. I gave my all to supporting and protecting my mentor from morning to evening. I chanted Nam-myoho-renge-kyo quietly all alone late at night. The mentor-disciple spirit I shared with my mentor was pure and noble. It is impossible for me to fully describe the experiences of my youth.

Youth need to cast aside pretense and empty posturing. Pretending to make effort while actually getting others to do all the hard work is to abuse the realm of faith. You need to start by setting an example yourself.

As a result of our recent triumphant campaigns nationwide, a whole new host of capable young people is emerging. This makes me very happy. I hope you will create a history of victory in every struggle for *kosen-rufu*, completely free of regret.

Mr. Toda said to the youth, with a sharp glimmer in his eye: "*Kosen-rufu* will advance as long as there is a single individual who is willing to fight, even if imprisoned or exiled. My goal is to foster such individuals of genuine commitment." I vowed that I would become one such individual. And I fulfilled my vow.

Fostering individuals of genuine commitment—this is the focus of the Soka Gakkai today. I am dedicating all my energies to this.

"Youth are to be regarded with respect," goes a famous Chinese saying, extolling the awesome promise of young people. Citing these words, Mr. Toda once said: "It is important that the disciples become great human beings. The fact that a mentor is described as great means that his disciples, his successors, have become great, thereby making him great." Mr. Toda regularly repeated those words to the members of the youth division.

Mentor and disciple are one. President Makiguchi's greatness was demonstrated by his disciple, President Toda. And I have proclaimed President Toda's greatness throughout the world.

Nothing Is Impossible

How can we bring forth our true potential? In his novel, *The Human Revolution*, Mr. Toda gave these words to the novel's hero, Gan: "When you make furious efforts, you'll come to display capabilities that you never had before—or, rather, I should say, capabilities or potential that you always possessed but never before tapped." That is absolutely true. We should never decide that something is impossible, buying into the belief, "I'll never be able to do that." The power of the entire universe is inherent in our lives. The Mystic Law is what draws that power out. Firmly decide, "I can do it!" When you do that, your determined prayers and actions will break through the walls of your self-imposed limitations.

On one occasion, Mr. Toda said to a young women's division member: "You should read Nichiren's writings more. Everything you need is written there." There is no greater loss than failing to read Nichiren's writings, because the answers to all of the most difficult problems in life and society are found therein. The

Daishonin's writings are filled with a compassion as deep as the ocean. They contain boundless wisdom, conviction and a burning, fighting spirit. The fundamental law governing all life and the universe is clearly revealed in these writings.

Prompt Communication

At another time, Mr. Toda said in a quiet, solemn voice: "You are not communicating enough. All sorts of things are happening. Why don't you bring them to my attention?" One report can save a life. On the other hand, a delayed report can cause trouble for many. This is something that, as top leaders, you need to keep constantly in mind.

Every day I carefully review reports from our precious members and communications from leading figures in various spheres of endeavor around the globe. I leave nothing untended but act on every one of them with lightning speed for the sake of the enduring success and development of our movement into the eternal future.

I can never forget Mr. Toda's assertion, "In any struggle, the side more solidly united is certain to triumph." And he urged all our members, "Let us aim to develop a magnificent state of life that will be praised, not by mere mortals, but by the Buddha!" In that spirit, let us boldly open a new stage of *kosen-rufu*.

From the August 2, 2004, Seikyo Shimbun

Fostering the Children,
the Successors of *Kosen-rufu*

JULY 28, 2004

This conference represents a gathering to deepen our understanding of Buddhism. It is a place to gain fresh inspiration in faith. With that in mind, I would like to speak to you a little again today.

Our summer training sessions and conferences are traditions going back to President Toda's day. Highly capable leaders gathered around Mr. Toda, where they fused their commitment, solidified their unity of purpose and made a fresh, energetic start. This annual rhythm of summer training sessions for leaders has played an important role in the Soka Gakkai's tremendous growth.

Action is crucial. You can hold all the conferences and discussions you want, but if they are not accompanied by action, then they are ultimately meaningless. It is vital to respond promptly and speedily to issues of concern, taking active measures to deal with them. The organization that can do this will prosper, grow and develop steadily into the future.

The Chinese writer Lu Xun wrote: "In short, mere words are not enough. Action is essential. Many people need to launch into action—the masses and the pioneers [in each field]."[1]

It is my hope that you, our leaders gathered here today, will take the initiative in stirring up a groundswell for a revolution in taking action toward the fresh growth and development of our movement.

Avoiding Complacency

"Any organization is always in danger of corruption and in need of reform from within."[2] These are the words of the twentieth-century poet T. S. Eliot. "Reform from within"—this is indispensable for the growth of any organization.

Washing away the sweat of the day leaves us feeling refreshed and invigorated; it's good for our health as well. In the same way, unceasing reform is vital in the organization for *kosen-rufu*. When leaders become self-satisfied, complacent and compromising, the organization soon stagnates. The organization must be constantly striving to improve and renew itself. Everything begins with the change in leaders' attitudes, leaders' determination.

An Interest in Buddhism

I'd like to speak to you a bit about the poet I mentioned earlier, Thomas Stearns Eliot. Born in the United States in 1888, he studied at Harvard University, the Sorbonne in Paris and Oxford in England. At Harvard, in particular, he showed an interest in Indian philosophy and Buddhism, and his studies strongly influenced his writing. His best-known poems are *The Waste Land* and *The Four Quartets*. He also wrote brilliant literary criticism, including *Notes Towards the Definition of Culture,* and was a Nobel laureate in literature. He died in London in January 1965.

Incidentally, I had the privilege of being invited to speak on two occasions at Harvard University, where Eliot studied.

[In 1991, President Ikeda delivered a speech at Harvard titled "The Age of Soft Power," and in 1993, a speech titled "Mahayana Buddhism and Twenty-first-Century Civilization."]

The World Is Our Stage

On the occasion of my second address at Harvard, the world-renowned economist and Harvard professor emeritus John Kenneth Galbraith served as a commentator. I will never forget his kindness. My wife and I enjoyed many friendly conversations with him, including a visit to his home on the outskirts of Boston [in 1993].

[A dialogue between SGI President Ikeda and Dr. Galbraith was serialized in the Soka Gakkai-related monthly magazine Ushio *from August 2003 through June 2004, under the title "Toward Creating a Great Age of Humanism" (English tentative title).]*

Dr. Galbraith wrote, "It is your friends who give you power."[3] Nothing is more powerful than friendship—friendship with people around the world, friendship with our neighbors and those in our community. The time has come for us to make even greater efforts to forge wonderful friendships with as many people as possible. I hope you will break through all inner barriers holding you back and reach out to others in a way that is enjoyable and most natural for you. A vast, unlimited stage stretches out before you.

Fostering Our Children

Across Japan, the Future Division Dynamic Growth Month [held during the school summer holidays] is under way. [*The future division includes the members of the elementary school division and the junior high and high school divisions.*] I would like to offer my deepest appreciation for the invaluable contributions of the future division leaders, the leaders of the student division who are offering guidance and advice to youngsters about higher education and the men's and women's division leaders who are responsible for supporting the future division. Thank you all for working so hard in this hot weather to foster the future division members.

If it were possible, I would like to see every single future division member go on to higher education. I'd like to see them go to university. A higher education opens up wonderful opportunities to develop one's potential to the fullest. Tuition and other expenses may be a problem for some, but there are many options such as night school and correspondence courses, and young people who are sufficiently motivated can work and study at the same time. There are innumerable ways to make it happen.

I would like to express my sincerest gratitude for the various kinds of support leaders are giving our future division members who aspire to attend college or university. My thanks as well to the members of the Soka Gakkai's education department. I appreciate your efforts in raising the precious young people who will carry on the Soka Gakkai's legacy.

The prime focus in our effort to nurture the future division members should be teaching them about faith. We should also strive to instill in them an awareness of the importance of school studies, friendship, reading, health and having appreciation for their parents. It is generally difficult for youngsters to shine in all these areas at the same time, but if their faith is sound and strong, all the efforts they make—whether in improving in their studies or in sport—will definitely come to bear fruit. Nothing is wasted in Buddhism.

In the family, it is also important to pass on the treasure of faith to our children, who are our successors. These practical efforts in daily life advance our movement for *kosen-rufu* and secure the path for the enduring prosperity of the Law.

The Truth Is Always Proven in the End

The German-American political philosopher Hannah Arendt, who was forced to flee Germany, the land of her birth, to escape persecution by the Nazis, declared that lasting deception is not possible. "There always comes the point beyond which lying becomes counterproductive,"[4] she wrote. History always demonstrates the truth in the end.

President Toda declared vigorously: "Soka Gakkai members have gathered together as followers of Nichiren Daishonin and are striving under the banner of *kosen-rufu*, because they are the emissaries of the Daishonin, the Buddha of the Latter Day of the Law. Therefore, anyone who slanders them is committing an offense that will plunge them into the hell of incessant suffering." What happens to those who persecute or defame Soka Gakkai members who are striving so earnestly for *kosen-rufu*? Mr. Toda declared that they will fall into the hell of incessant suffering.

Nichiren Daishonin was equally severe.

In "The Selection of the Time," he cited a passage from the Great Teacher Dengyo, "Those who slander him [a person who upholds the Lotus Sutra] will be committing a fault that will condemn them to the hell of incessant suffering" (WND-1, 583).

In "Many in Body, One in Mind," Nichiren wrote, "The Japanese people will slander the Lotus Sutra more than ever, and all of them will fall into the hell of incessant suffering" (WND-1, 618).

And in "Questions and Answers about Embracing the Lotus Sutra," he asserted, "A person who despises, looks down on, hates, envies, or holds a grudge against those who read and embrace the Lotus Sutra will fall into the great citadel of the Avichi hell [i.e., the hell of incessant suffering] after he dies" (WND-1, 61).

Since this is so, we can advance with confidence and high spirits, certain in the knowledge that we will ultimately triumph.

The Growth of Youth

While teaching young people about the essence of Buddhism, Mr. Toda said: "It pleases a mentor not in the least to have his disciples massage his shoulders and take care of him. What makes a mentor happy is if his disciples understand even one of the things he is trying to teach them."

When we follow our mentor's guidance and instruction, making our hearts one with our mentor, we can grow into great and capable individuals.

"I wish to dedicate my life to *kosen-rufu*," said Mr. Toda. "I have not the slightest interest in personal gain or benefit." This was his strict and unwavering attitude in every situation. It is the model of a true Buddhist and revolutionary.

A Noble Gathering of Buddhas

The organization is the Soka Gakkai's lifeblood. Mr. Toda valued it above all, proclaiming, "The Soka Gakkai organization is more precious than my own life." This short and concise statement expresses his deepest conviction and belief.

The organization of *kosen-rufu* is not simply a gathering of people. It is a gathering of Buddhas. The Soka Gakkai pulses with the life of Buddhahood of the entire universe. That is its essence.

Anyone who ridicules our organization, exploits it for personal gain or tries to destroy it is committing the serious offense known in Buddhism as disrupting the harmonious unity of believers.

Mr. Toda instructed sternly: "Buddhist compassion entails fighting against traitors and ingrates. The Soka Gakkai is the most joyful and harmonious realm in the universe. We cannot permit devilish forces to destroy it. We must never let even a single individual with evil intentions come anywhere near our noble organization!"

Mr. Toda also told leaders, "When you, the leaders, embrace your leadership positions with a real sense of joy and appreciation, the organization will achieve even greater results."

In addition, he addressed the following points of guidance to leaders:

"Arrogance in a leader is a sign of foolishness, ignorance, lack of character and weak faith."

"Leaders are the servants of the members. Members shouldn't have to go about trying to curry favor with leaders. I will dismiss without fail any leader who is arrogant or conceited."

"Our organization exists for the sake of *kosen-rufu*. If its leaders become arrogant, sitting back and taking advantage of the organization, the Gakkai will collapse."

Since you are the top leaders of the Soka Gakkai, I want to stress these points to you with special firmness.

An Unparalleled Life

Lasting happiness is not to be found on the path of gaining worldly power or acclaim. Those who strive the hardest for the Law, for others and for society will enjoy the greatest happiness. This is the strict Buddhist law of cause and effect.

Soka Gakkai activities represent the path of attaining Buddha-hood. When we link arms with our friends and walk that path together, brilliant flowers of hope and prosperity will blossom.

The benefits all of you are accumulating are infinite and immeasurable, and they will flow on without fail to your children and descendants throughout successive generations.

A life dedicated to *kosen-rufu* is unparalleled. How wonderful it is to walk that path together with our friends. Being alive itself is a source of joy.

I hope that you will live out your days with this spirit and attain lives of immense victory.

You have achieved a magnificent accomplishment for *kosen-rufu*. How delighted President Makiguchi and President Toda would surely be.

Striving is happiness. Not making an effort leads nowhere. Without striving, we cannot improve ourselves, experience joy or realize inner growth.

Let's all remember to pay careful attention to our health at all times.

Our network of Soka humanism has spread to 190 countries and territories [*as of 2009, the number has grown to 192*], and we have members in Cuba in the beautiful Caribbean as well as in the vast nation of Russia. The entire world is now our stage. Let's continue our spirited effort to expand our grand movement of peace and culture across the globe.

From the August 3, 2004, Seikyo Shimbun

NOTES

1 Translated from Chinese. Lu Xun, *Lu Xun quanji* (The Complete Works of Lu Xun) (Beijing: Renmin Wenxue Chubanshe, 1996), vol. 6, p. 102.

2 T. S. Eliot, *Christianity and Culture: The Idea of a Christian Society* and *Notes towards the Definition of Culture* (New York: Harcourt, Brace and Company, 1949), p. 38.

3 John Kenneth Galbraith, *A Life in Our Times: Memoirs* (Boston: Houghton Mifflin Company, 1981), p. 400.

4 Hannah Arendt, "Lying in Politics," in *Crises of the Republic* (New York: Harcourt, Brace and Company, 1972), p. 7.

The Lifeblood of Faith
Lies in the Practice of *Shakubuku*

JULY 29, 2004

The aim of Nichiren Buddhism is the happiness of all humankind. That is the purpose of *shakubuku*, of spreading the correct teaching. It is a compassionate struggle to lead those who are suffering to enlightenment. The lifeblood of faith in Nichiren Buddhism does not exist apart from the practice of *shakubuku*.

The *shakubuku* spirit is the Gakkai's foundation. The Great Teacher T'ien-t'ai declared, "The Lotus Sutra is the teaching of shakubuku, the refutation of the provisional doctrines" (WND-1, 394). Embracing these golden words, the Daishonin himself carried out *shakubuku* with great vigor. Throughout his life, he consistently refuted false doctrines and erroneous teachings.

Leaders devoid of the *shakubuku* spirit are not followers of the Daishonin. They cannot hope to receive the true benefits of practicing faith.

Nichiren wrote: "Buddhism is like the body, and society like the shadow. When the body bends, so does the shadow" (WND-1, 1039). We will be doing the very opposite of what we should be doing if, as a result of trying too hard to accommodate others or gain acceptance in society, we compromise our fundamental spirit. This is something we must remember.

The times and society are constantly changing. It's only natural that the structure and format of Gakkai activities will also change. However, no matter where you are or whom you're with, it is crucial to speak out against error and injustice and give people a correct understanding of our movement. We must never lose the spirit to "refute the erroneous and reveal the true."

Undaunted by Persecution

Those who propagate the Mystic Law in the Latter Day of the Law are certain to experience persecution. The Lotus Sutra asserts this quite clearly, saying that people will "curse and speak ill of us" (LS13, 193), and "Since hatred and jealousy toward this sutra abound even when the Thus Come One is in the world, how much more will this be so after his passing?" (LS10, 164). Nichiren quoted these and similar passages repeatedly, and he stated that those who did not meet with persecution were not true votaries of the Lotus Sutra but impostors.

[Nichiren wrote: "Understand then that the votary who practices the Lotus Sutra exactly as the Buddha teaches will without fail be attacked by the three powerful enemies" (WND-1, 395), and "Without tribulation there would be no votary of the Lotus Sutra" (WND-1, 33).]

In our times, only the Soka Gakkai is being criticized, maligned and persecuted for upholding the Law. The priesthood, which is utterly lacking in the shakubuku spirit, has never been persecuted for promoting kosen-rufu.

President Toda proclaimed with a mighty lion's roar, "The Soka Gakkai is the king of the religious world!" He left these words for the youth of future generations.

Let's advance vigorously along the great and honorable path of propagating Nichiren Buddhism as champions of philosophy, of peace and of humanity!

Sincerity Is Crucial

Mr. Toda's fervent wish was to have people throughout Japan and the entire world read the *Seikyo Shimbun*. Nichiren declared solemnly: "It is through the use of words and letters that the Buddha saves living beings" (WND-2, 6), and "If one rejects the use of words and letters, then how can the Buddha's work be done?" (WND-2, 6–7). The *Seikyo Shimbun* is a newspaper dedicated to the ideals of Buddhist humanism. It is a paper that carries the words of *kosen-rufu*.

Expanding the number of people who read and subscribe to the *Seikyo Shimbun* is equivalent to the expansion of *kosen-rufu*. It is the Buddha's noble work that corresponds to *shakubuku*. Accordingly, everyone who joins in this endeavor will reap benefit in direct proportion to his or her efforts. Your own frontiers of *kosen-rufu* will expand. Above all, you will feel energized. You know better than anyone how true this is.

I hope that, as the top leaders of our organization, you will take even greater initiative in this effort, sharing with your fellow members your experiences and joy in promoting the *Seikyo Shimbun*. Please humbly and sincerely encourage everyone to do his or her best, too. Let them know you are chanting for them and will do anything you can to support them.

Serious dedication and genuine sincerity are the most essential qualities for leaders. The organization is propelled by the determination and actions of leaders. I would like to reaffirm this point with all of you today.

Happiness in Our Final Years

Mr. Toda also used to say frequently, "The last years of our life are crucial." He remarked: "Happiness in life isn't determined half-way through. It is the last few years before we die that are decisive. A state of genuine happiness is something we only attain in our final years." This was certainly true of Mr. Toda's life.

No matter how happy you may be along the way, if your final years are full of suffering, then your life will end in misfortune and defeat. On the other hand, if your final years are happy, all your past hardships are transformed into wonderful memories.

Mr. Toda therefore told the youth to valiantly struggle and undergo hardships in propagating Nichiren Buddhism until they themselves achieve such a sublime state of life, never forgetting the Buddhist spirit of selfless dedication to spreading the Law.

Today, in every field of endeavor, we see the growth of outstanding Soka Gakkai youth. I receive regular reports from talented and gifted members active in numerous fields such as business, education, the arts, entertainment and sports. This makes me very happy. My greatest joy is to see young people, radiant with the light of intense effort, developing into wonderful human beings.

We now have a magnificent array of capable new leaders whose job it will be to construct a new era. I wish to proclaim this to all of you today.

Building the Foundation of Happiness in Youth

Many women's and young women's division leaders are participating in today's meeting. As an expression of my sincerest praise for your dedicated efforts, I'd like to talk a little bit about the

French philosopher and social activist Simone Weil, because all of you, too, are philosophers of peace.

True Buddhism is open to the world. A life of value creation seeks to sweep away walls and boundaries and learn from the wisdom of all kinds of people everywhere around the globe.

Simone Weil was born in 1909 in Paris. Her father was a physician. At the age of sixteen, she entered the famous secondary school Lycée Henri IV, wishing to study the thought of the philosopher Alain [pseudonym of Emile Chartier], who taught there. As a teacher, Alain encouraged his students to read as many good books as possible. He also had them constantly writing reports and critiques to develop their ability to think. The young Weil studied avidly and wrote voluminously. She engaged her mentor with the full force of her intellect. For his part, Alain was very pleased with his student's rapid progress, and he continued to challenge her mind and train her rigorously.

The training of our youth is the foundation for all future happiness. Weil's encounter with the philosophy of Alain was her starting point in life.

Putting the Students First

After graduating from the French university École Normal Supérieure, the twenty-two-year-old Weil became an instructor in philosophy at a national girls secondary school. She spared no effort for her students. A visiting school inspector was startled to see that Weil's students had a firm grasp of her difficult course material. Weil gave free private instruction to her students who were struggling with their studies.

Actually, Weil was not physically strong. She suffered from

constant severe headaches, but that could not keep her from carrying out her mission and duties as an educator.

A former student said of her, with love and respect, "She always put us before her own comfort and personal interests."[1]

As Courageous As Joan of Arc

Simone Weil always identified with those who were suffering, and she lived her life accordingly. Never giving her poor health a second thought, she worked among farmers and fishermen. Though she had her own job as a teacher, she could not ignore the sufferings of people toiling under adverse conditions. She made time in her busy schedule to teach them about philosophy and other subjects. They admired and respected her, feeling ennobled and uplifted by her presence. Weil later took a leave of absence from her teaching position to work in a factory, hiding her real identity.

Renowned as a fierce champion of the oppressed, she had a powerful empathy for the sufferings of people around the world as well as the courage to stand up and fight against injustice. These qualities animated her entire being.

There were people in the region where she taught high school whose welfare was deplorably neglected by the government, so Weil became their staunch advocate. As a result, she was attacked by certain sectors of the mass media with slanderous accusations and malicious lies. But instead of silencing her, these attacks only prompted her to speak out more vocally until she had won better treatment for the poor of the region. For her valor, one of her friends compared her to Joan of Arc, France's courageous champion and beacon of hope.

Protecting Spiritual Values

Simone Weil was keenly aware of the inherently devilish nature of power. She declared that tyranny "kills spiritual values."[2] This is very true, and it is why the public needs to keep a careful watch at all times over those who wield power and authority.

Weil devoted her life to the struggle against tyrannical power. When the Spanish Civil War began in 1936, she hurried to Spain and volunteered for the anti-fascist republican forces. During World War II, she joined the French Resistance in England to fight against the Nazi occupation of her homeland.

She was willing to risk her life for her beliefs. She could not bear to be inactive as long as her fellow citizens, her fellow human beings, were suffering and struggling. She could not bear to see friends in adversity or hardship.

Rushing to the aid of friends in need without a thought for oneself—this calls to mind our women's and young women's division members.

There Is Only One Truth!

Simone Weil died in 1943 of tuberculosis and malnutrition. She was only thirty-four years old.

Her main writings include *Gravity and Grace* (1947), *Oppression and Liberty* (1955) and *The Need for Roots* (1953). Like these, most of her writings were edited and published posthumously. Her life and thought had a tremendous effect on other writers and the world in general after her death.

During her lifetime, deep-rooted prejudice against women taking an active role in society still prevailed. Weil, however, refused to let this stop her and cultivated strong friendships and warm alliances.

She also declared that there was only one truth, one justice.[3] It is under the banner of truth that people unite. Let us therefore advance with supreme confidence on the great path to world peace!

In closing, I would especially like to share with our youth division members some words from a letter that Weil wrote to one of her students: "The important thing is not to damage your life. That is why you need to forge yourself."[4]

Now is the time to train yourselves. It is crucial that you build a self that can never be defeated.

From its pioneering days, the Soka Gakkai spirit has always been to take on every challenge, fully prepared for persecution.

To remain true to one's convictions, to walk the path of mentor and disciple, the path of comrades in faith—this is the greatest possible life.

My friends, live courageous lives like Simone Weil and Joan of Arc!

Together let's lead lives of supreme happiness to the very end.

From the August 4, 2004, Seikyo Shimbun

NOTES

1 Translated from French. Simone Pétrement, *La vie de Simone Weil* (The Life of Simone Weil) (Paris: Fayard, 1973), p. 160.
2 Translated from French. Simone Weil, "Réflexions en vue d'un bilan," *Écrits historiques et politiques,* in *Oeuvres complètes,* edited by André A. Devaux and Florence de Lussy (Paris: Gallimard, 1960), vol. 2, p. 113.
3 Translated from Japanese. Simone Weil, *Shimonu Veyu chosaku-shu* (Collected Writings of Simone Weil) (Tokyo: Shunju-sha, 1993), vol. 2, p. 519.
4 Ibid., p. 173.

Live With Eternity, Happiness, True Self and Purity

JULY 30, 2004

Next year, 2005, will mark the seventy-fifth anniversary of the Soka Gakkai's founding, while in 2010 we will celebrate our eightieth anniversary. I'd like to suggest that we make these years our new targets. As you know, in Buddhism the number eight has the meaning "to open." The year of our eightieth anniversary will also mark the fiftieth anniversary of my inauguration as third president and of my first overseas trip for the sake of worldwide *kosen-rufu*. Time passes so quickly.

Aiming toward 2005 and then 2010, let's build an unprecedented citadel of Soka. Let's construct an indomitable, ever-victorious organization.

As we advance our movement for *kosen-rufu*, we are certain to be protected by the positive forces of the universe. Now is the time for us to firmly consolidate our network for peace. Youth are the key. We need to extend our network further, to embrace even more young people and lay a solid foundation for the second stage of the Soka Gakkai's development. This is the important mission of the youth division.

I am praying that the youth will stand up and, with even greater vigor, demonstrate superb leadership in promoting *kosen-rufu* in the area of their responsibility.

Leading the Way Toward Victory

Our seventy-fifth anniversary next year also draws a correlation to the five or seven characters of the Mystic Law (Nam-myoho-renge-kyo). [*The phrase* Myoho-renge-kyo *consists of five Chinese characters;* Nam-myoho-renge-kyo *consists of seven.*] In this deeply significant year, the key to all victory will be prayer first and foremost—steadfast, earnest prayer.

I call on you to advance in high spirits and win through everything with outstanding leadership like that demonstrated by Chuko K'ung-ming [*or Zhuge Liang, the famous ancient Chinese military strategist and prime minister*].

And male leaders—particularly the leaders of the men's division—need to make even more earnest and sincere efforts and show the highest respect for our women's and young women's division members. From now on, any organization that fails to value women is bound to be left behind and fall into decline. I say this again and again because it is so important for our male leaders to take this truth deeply to heart.

The Importance of Practice and Study

Buddhist study is absolutely vital. It is the very heart of the Soka Gakkai. Some have suggested that the fundamental spiritual decay afflicting the priesthood can be attributed to their failure to study Buddhist doctrine.

Shakyamuni's final words were "Rely on the Law and not upon persons" (WND-1, 109). In the Soka Gakkai, the Law is always our center, and the writings of Nichiren Daishonin our foundation. The Soka Gakkai's tradition has always been intense and thorough Buddhist study. The Daishonin wrote: "Exert yourself in the two ways of practice and study. Without practice and study, there can be no Buddhism" (WND-1, 386).

The youth division is crucial. It is essential that they develop a solid understanding of Buddhist tenets during their youth. Toward that end, let's continue to actively promote Buddhist study, with the study department taking the lead.

Spiritual Champions

The time is approaching for new personnel appointments in the Soka Gakkai organization in Japan. My best wishes to everyone who will be taking on a new responsibility or moving to a new arena. At the same time, some will be handing over their positions to others. We all grow older, and it's only natural that we won't be able to stay in the same position forever. Everything is in a state of continual flux and change. What matters is to establish and maintain a life-condition of eternity, happiness, true self and purity, to attain the unchanging spirit of a champion. As Nichiren wrote, it is the heart that is important.

Though your position may change, your spirit, your attitude should remain unchanged. Never regress. Wherever you are, wherever you go, encourage and praise others, always continuing to move forward for the sake of *kosen-rufu* and your fellow members. That is the Soka Gakkai spirit.

I also hope you will dedicate yourself to fostering your juniors. There is no greater source of pride for a senior than having raised many fine, capable people.

Those Who Chant Nam-myoho-renge-kyo Have Infinite Hope

In April 1979, twenty-five years ago, I stepped down as the third president of the Soka Gakkai. But whether I was president or not, I did not change. I visited the homes of individual members who had worked hard to pioneer our movement. I wrote letters and brief messages of encouragement to those I couldn't meet personally, and sometimes I even played the piano to encourage members. I fought on tirelessly, never relaxing in my efforts, and built the Soka Gakkai into the international organization it is today with one thought in mind: bringing happiness to our members.

It is important to keep moving forward, one step at a time, like a steadily flowing river, never halting or standing still, never hesitating or retreating.

Those who have faith, those who chant Nam-myoho-renge-kyo strongly and consistently, those who are dedicated to *kosen-rufu*, no matter what circumstances they may find themselves in, can open a path of limitless hope.

If we base our lives on Buddhism, we will never be at an impasse.

Looking Forward Positively to the Future

Today, Japan's birth rate is declining, and the population is aging rapidly. It is commonly noted that most organizations are worried about their future. But let's look on the bright side of these developments. If there are fewer children, let's put more energy into raising each one to become an immensely capable individual. If there are more elderly people, let's work to create an environment where they can make active, positive contributions to society.

The World Is Our Stage

The Soka Gakkai is not limited to the small nation of Japan. The entire world is our stage.

The members of the SGI-USA have been making great strides in introducing people to Nichiren Buddhism. The members of SGI-South Korea have opened a magnificent new headquarters building. Members in Malaysia, Singapore and other Asian nations are making outstanding contributions to their local communities. In Europe, Latin America, Oceania and Africa, our members have won wide understanding and high expectations for the SGI's humanistic movement.

There are some 6.3 billion people on this planet. The task of spreading Nichiren Buddhism around the globe has only just begun. With that in mind, I have been taking steps on every level for the future. We are now producing a steady stream of extremely capable people who can hold their own in the global arena. I also plan to continue taking leadership for worldwide *kosen-rufu* with renewed energy.

Aiming toward next year, 2005, and May 3 of 2010, the year we celebrate our eightieth anniversary, let's strive to achieve brilliant victory in our lives and together greet these anniversaries in good health and high spirits.

From the August 5, 2004, Seikyo Shimbun

Shine the Most Brilliantly
Where You Are

JULY 31, 2004

President Toda was fond of white lilies—the flower that is the women's division symbol. White lilies, blooming beautifully, pure, refined and lovely. What flower could better represent the Soka Gakkai women's division?

In one of his writings, the Great Teacher Dengyo [the founder of the Japanese Tendai school of Buddhism] asked, "What is the treasure of the nation?" His answer was that those who seek the correct teaching of Buddhism and courageously practice it are the true treasure of the nation.

[In his work titled The Regulations for Students of the Mountain School, Dengyo wrote, "A mind that seeks the way is a treasure; those who possess this seeking mind are the treasure of the nation."]

The members of the women's division, striving tirelessly for kosen-rufu, are the most precious treasure of the nation and, indeed, of the entire world. I commend you all for your valiant efforts, day in and day out. Thank you!

The young women's division members are also demonstrating remarkable growth. They have truly developed into people of wonderful talent and ability.

The path of *kosen-rufu* is the path to attaining genuine happiness and fulfillment in life. I hope you will all advance straight ahead along this sure path and live out your lives together with the Soka Gakkai. Therein lies a youth of unsurpassed vibrance, brilliance and triumph.

The Greatest Honor

The ancient Greek philosopher Aristotle wrote: "Men who are well-born are thought worthy of honor, and so are those who enjoy power or wealth. . . . [B]ut in truth the good man alone is to be honored."[1] True honor is not a matter of birth or power or wealth. Let us give the highest honors to those who are upright and honest. This was Aristotle's cry.

Next year, 2005, will be the seventy-fifth anniversary of the Soka Gakkai's founding. To commemorate that milestone, we are planning to bestow the highest awards and honors on members who have made outstanding contributions to *kosen-rufu* over the years. It is our sincere members, leading noble lives of mission, who deserve to be honored above all.

The English poet John Milton observed, "For it often falls out that among the Commons there are many far better and wiser men than among the Lords."[2] This is absolutely true. The ordinary people are great and worthy of respect.

And the strongest alliance of ordinary people who possess infinite merit and wisdom is the Soka Gakkai.

The Truth Must Prevail

My mentor, President Toda, called out passionately to the youth: "Only by winning can justice be upheld. We must never let justice be defeated." The Mystic Law is the ultimate force for justice. It is the power source for indestructible victory.

We must ensure that what is true and correct in the light of reason is actualized in society.

Therefore, we who embrace Nichiren Buddhism must definitely triumph.

If the truth does not prevail, if the truth is permitted to be defeated, then justice will not be served.

The great French writer Victor Hugo envisaged a time when there would be "no struggle but the struggle for good, for beauty, for greatness, for justice, for truth, and the struggle to overcome obstacles and seek the ideal."[3]

Life is a struggle. Existence is a struggle with reality in all its aspects. And in the midst of that ongoing struggle, we of the SGI are carrying out an unsurpassed challenge to actualize our mission. This is *kosen-rufu*.

Kosen-rufu is a struggle to lead all humanity to peace and happiness, a struggle to illuminate the world with the light of the humanistic philosophy of Nichiren Buddhism. It is a struggle to bring forth to its fullest the positive potential and inherent goodness within all human beings.

We, the members who champion this sublime cause, must not be defeated under any circumstances. We must win without fail. Victory holds the key to hope, progress, happiness and a bright future.

Buddhism is about being victorious. Once we engage in a struggle, it is vital that we win ultimate victory by employing the best strategies and the best possible leadership lineup. This is the Soka Gakkai spirit.

Leadership positions in the Soka Gakkai are positions of responsibility. As leaders, it is important that we strive wholeheartedly to fulfill the duties of our respective positions and successfully carry out our mission. The important thing is to advance with sincere and single-minded dedication in line with our commitment. That is the key to making our inherent qualities shine, to revealing our truest and highest potential. As long as leaders are concerned about appearances and the praise of others, they aren't genuine leaders. Their actions will remain self-centered. The primary goal and focus of our organization are to realize *kosen-rufu* and to enable our members to grow in faith. That is why we have leaders.

"I'll Carry Out My Mission Here!"

President Toda, who endured almost two years in prison for his opposition to Japan's militarist authorities during World War II, once reflected: "When I was first placed in prison, it was torture as I kept wondering, 'When will I be able to go home?' 'When will they let me out?' But once I decided, 'I'm here for life,' it was unexpectedly easy."

What we see here is a subtle difference in mind-set, in attitude. It is this subtle difference on which everything hinges, for better or for worse. Strong are those who, no matter how adverse their circumstances, no matter how difficult their situation, decide to carry out their mission right where they are.

That is the key—to be courageous and engage life head-on. That is the ultimate essence of Nichiren Buddhism, which teaches unending advancement.

The Soka Gakkai's Struggle

Nichiren wrote, "If they [devils] did not [arise], there would be no way of knowing that this is the correct teaching" (WND-1, 501).

President Makiguchi said, "We must ask which of the followers of Nichiren Shoshu until now have been assailed by the three obstacles and four devils."[4] He sought to point out that no one in the priesthood was fighting against the three obstacles and four devils, which indicated that they weren't practicing the correct teaching.

On June 27, 1943, the priesthood summoned President Makiguchi and Mr. Toda and, in the presence of the high priest, instructed the Soka Gakkai to accept the Shinto talisman that the government required all Japanese to worship. In this way, the priests, fearful of government persecution, tried to coerce the Soka Gakkai into committing slander of the Law.

Mr. Makiguchi flatly refused and departed. The next day [June 28], he met with the high priest once more and strongly urged him to remonstrate with the government authorities. Just eight days later [on July 6], Mr. Makiguchi was arrested by the Special Higher Police [as was Mr. Toda].

An indignant Mr. Makiguchi said to Mr. Toda: "What I lament is not the ruin of a single school but the destruction of an entire nation. I fear the grief the Daishonin would surely feel. Isn't this precisely the time to remonstrate with the government? What are they [the priesthood] afraid of?"[5]

To protect themselves, the cowardly priesthood trampled on and abandoned Nichiren's teachings. Only the Soka Gakkai has battled against the three obstacles and four devils and the three powerful enemies. Only the Soka Gakkai has endured persecution and triumphed over every obstacle. We must never lose the courage to speak out for the truth, unafraid of persecution, for the sake of peace and the welfare of humanity.

Ideas Lead the World

I wonder if today's youth division members have heard of French President Charles de Gaulle? He was a great statesman and former general who was regarded as the liberator of his homeland. Former U.S. Secretary of State Henry Kissinger, with whom I conducted a dialogue, recalled that whenever he was in the same room as de Gaulle, he felt as if the center of gravity moved with the French leader. Such was the commanding presence de Gaulle exuded.

During World War II, in a lecture at Oxford University in England, de Gaulle declared that ideas lead the world. It is not military or economic might that guides the world, but ideas. Human beings live by ideas.

We of the SGI have the great humanistic teaching of Buddhism, we have faith, we have Nam-myoho-renge-kyo, and we have the writings of Nichiren Daishonin. These are what make us strong. Let us advance with confidence and pride.

De Gaulle proclaimed, "Our cohesion is complete and will never crack, no matter what may happen."[6] His words resounded with unshakable conviction.

Unity Is the Key to Victory

Never form factions—this was President Toda's injunction.

De Gaulle fought valiantly against the storms of fascism raging across Europe. He declared with absolute conviction: "We must redouble our efforts to attain victory,"[7] and "Nothing great can be accomplished without passion."[8]

Even after Paris fell and the French government capitulated to the Nazis, de Gaulle did not give up. Asserting "I am France," he declared he would continue to fight. He fled to England, where he set up a government in exile and persisted in the struggle for the liberation of his nation.

Burning passion—that alone reaches people's hearts; it ignites a flame of courage within them.

Let us, too, lead our lives with great passion burning in our hearts. Our daily chanting of Nam-myoho-renge-kyo represents the highest form of passion.

Leaders Need Philosophy

The French essayist and author Madame de Staël wrote, "It has often been said that religion is necessary for the lower orders, and I think it is easy to prove that persons of elevated rank have still more need of it."[9]

Those in leadership positions have a special need for religion, and nations need moral principles more urgently than individuals do, says Madame de Staël with the keenness so characteristic of French thinkers. That is because a people whose leaders lack a profound spirituality are unfortunate indeed.

De Gaulle declared he would fight until the day of final victory. In the same way, let us advance courageously together on our path, the lofty path of *kosen-rufu*.

From the August 6, 2004, Seikyo Shimbun

Notes

1 Aristotle, *Nicomachean Ethics* (Bk. IV: Ch. 3), in *Introduction to Aristotle*, edited by Richard McKeon (New York: The Modern Library, 1947), p. 385.
2 John Milton, *The Works of John Milton* (New York: Columbia University Press, 1932), vol. 7, p. 389.

3 Translated from French. Victor Hugo, "Anniversaire de la Révolution de 1848," *Pendant l'Exil 1852–1870*, in *Actes et Paroles* (Paris: Albin Michel, 1938), vol. 2, p. 109.

4 At the 1942 general meeting of the Soka Kyoiku Gakkai (forerunner of the Soka Gakkai).

5 Translated from Japanese. Josei Toda, "Soka Gakkai no rekishi to kakushin" (The History and Conviction of the Soka Gakkai), in *Toda Josei zenshu* (Collected Writings of Josei Toda) (Tokyo: Seikyo Shimbunsha, 1983), vol. 3, p. 107.

6 Translated from French. Charles de Gaulle, *Mémoires de Guerre: L' Unité, 1942–1944* (Paris: Librairie Plon, 1956), p. 374.

7 Ibid., p. 132.

8 Translated from French. Charles de Gaulle, *Mémoires de Guerre: L' Appel, 1940–1942* (Paris: Librairie Plon, 1954), p. 672.

9 Baroness de Staël, *Considerations on the Principal Events of the French Revolution* (London: Baldwin, Cradock, and Joy, 1821), vol. 2, p. 316.

Don't Waste a Single Day

AUGUST 1, 2004

Buddhism is the way of ceaseless self-improvement and absolute happiness. This way can only be attained through earnest Buddhist practice. No matter how famous, powerful or wealthy one may be, unless one understands the fundamental path of life that is the Mystic Law, one cannot realize a state of indestructible happiness. This path of everlasting victory and good fortune is the very path along which the Soka Gakkai is advancing.

Nichiren Daishonin wrote, "Thus within the tents of command they were able to devise strategies that assured victory a thousand miles away" (WND-2, 391). The Soka Gakkai must not be divided and unorganized. It is important for leaders to exchange opinions, draw up detailed plans and take appropriate action. We need to establish clear goals, chant for them and advance with unity of purpose. That is the formula for victory.

Illuminating the World With Peace and Culture

I received a report from Danny Nagashima, general director of the SGI-USA, informing me that a new SGI community center opened in New Orleans, Louisiana [on July 31, 2004]. The city of New

Orleans has commemorated this event by issuing a citation lauding the contributions to world peace made by the SGI members in New Orleans and me as president of our global movement. This is yet another sign of the trust that people of nations around the world place in the SGI as an international organization promoting peace, culture and education. I would like to share this honor with all our members.

[In March 2004, to commemorate the thirtieth anniversary of President and Mrs. Ikeda's visit to New Orleans, the city established a Daisaku and Kaneko Ikeda Friendship Grove that includes oak trees dedicated to the first three Soka Gakkai presidents—Tsunesaburo Makiguchi, Josei Toda and Daisaku Ikeda.]

I also received news from President Masao Yokota of the Soka Gakkai–affiliated Boston Research Center for the 21st Century that the total number of college and university courses in the United States in which academic works published by the center have been or are being used as textbooks and supplemental teaching materials has now climbed to more than two hundred. They include courses taught at such prestigious universities as Harvard, Columbia and Stanford.

[A number of these works contain forewords or articles by President Ikeda, who is also the founder of the Boston Research Center.]

[In a recent interview with Mr. Yokota,] Dr. William McLennan Jr., dean of the Office for Religious Life at Stanford University, remarked on the Soka Gakkai's resistance to persecution by Japan's militarist and religious authorities during World War II and its subsequent postwar growth. He described our history of constant reform as the key to our success in building an international organization dedicated to peace. He further voiced the hope that other traditions would follow our example and move out into the larger world.

Leading thinkers see things clearly; they are open and broad-minded. A society in which people properly recognize and value the truth has a bright and positive future. On the other hand, a society in which people are jealous of greatness and malign virtuous people is destined to decay.

Building an Enduring Bridge of Friendship

I have built numerous bridges throughout the world—bridges linking the hearts of people, transcending cultural and ideological differences. Realizing Japan-China friendship in particular has been one of my most cherished commitments and goals.

Three decades ago, Chinese Premier Zhou Enlai told me that he, too, hoped for the speedy conclusion of a treaty of peace and friendship between China and Japan. That was on a cold December 5, 1974, in the Beijing hospital where he was undergoing medical treatment.

I met then-Vice Premier Deng Xiaoping the following year, on April 16, 1975. At the time, the signing of the Japan-China Peace and Friendship Treaty had been held up because of what was referred to as the "hegemony issue." We earnestly discussed ways to overcome this problem. I did everything I could in my capacity as Soka Gakkai president to pave the way forward.

[The Joint Communiqué of the Government of Japan and the Government of the People's Republic of China, signed by the two nations on Sept. 29, 1972, contains a clause stating the signatories' opposition to hegemony. Known as the "anti-hegemony clause," it reads in part:"Neither of the two countries should seek hegemony in the Asia-Pacific region and each is opposed to efforts by any other country or group of countries to establish such hegemony." Some in the Japanese government, however, wished to have this clause removed from the peace and friendship treaty,

thereby hindering its conclusion. The signing eventually went ahead with its inclusion.]

After surmounting various obstacles, the treaty was finally signed in August 1978. Premier Zhou had already passed away [in 1976]. The realization of the treaty was a great accomplishment that would never have come to fruition without the efforts of his successor, Deng Xiaoping. This year marks the hundredth anniversary of the latter's birth [on Aug. 22, 1904]. Today, China is showing dynamic growth and development. I can just imagine how happy Deng would be.

Let us strive to make this golden bridge of friendship between Japan and China even stronger and more enduring.

[The online edition of China's Renmin Ribao *(People's Daily) ran a special series to commemorate the centennial of Deng Xiaoping's birth. In a tribute titled "Comrade Deng Xiaoping and the China-Japan Peace and Friendship Treaty," China-Japan Friendship Association Senior Advisor Zhang Xiangshan wrote: "On April 16, 1975, Comrade Deng Xiaoping met with Japan's Soka Gakkai President Daisaku Ikeda. . . . On that occasion, Comrade Deng stated his opinion that, from a historical point of view, the inclusion of the anti-hegemony clause in the treaty would be beneficial and was indeed necessary for the improvement of Japan's relations with the nations of Asia and the Pacific. . . . Comrade Deng entrusted President Ikeda with a message for Japan's then-Prime Minister Miki. The message was that he had great expectations that the Japanese leader would act courageously and decisively, and that he believed firmly upholding the principles of the Joint Communiqué would be advantageous to the peoples of both nations."*

In addition, Chinese academics have demonstrated a strong interest in President Ikeda's efforts to promote China-Japan friendship and his contributions to world peace. As a reflection of this, Daisaku Ikeda research groups and institutes have been established at a number of leading universities throughout China, including Beijing University, Hunan Normal University, Anhui University and Zhaoqing University.]

Refusing To Condone Injustice

Here I would like to share with you the words of the renowned Chinese writer Lu Xun.

Lu Xun was always a staunch ally of the people. He relentlessly attacked those who harassed and oppressed them. Angered by some irresponsible journalists and commentators whose articles criticized the weak in society, he wrote in condemnation:

> If one utters not a word, if one issues not a single protest against the prevailing forces of darkness and just criticizes the weak while assuming an air of self-righteousness, then I am compelled to say—I cannot keep myself from saying—one is nothing but an accomplice to murder.[1]

He denounces those who get on their high horse to censure the vulnerable and disadvantaged while failing to address the fundamental problems that give rise to the social injustices that are the cause of their plight. Such individuals are not qualified to be journalists; their actions aid and abet the oppressors, making them little better than criminals themselves, he declared.

Tsunesaburo Makiguchi, the Soka Gakkai's first president, said, "Cowards who cannot say what needs to be said are not qualified to be the Daishonin's disciples."

A passionate refusal to condone injustice—this fighting spirit must be the Soka Gakkai spirit.

Creating the Cause for Our Next Victory

Lu Xun also wrote: "After a minor victory, many grow drunk on their triumph, let themselves relax and forget to press their advantage. This invites the enemy to find a gap in their defenses and attempt another assault."[2] To never lose sight of our adversaries—this is the key to eternal victory.

In any organization, when the top leaders grow negligent or arrogant, they create an opening for devilish functions to take advantage.

When we win, that is precisely the time to create the cause for our next victory. It is important to transform the joy of victory into the energy to press ahead vigorously in our fresh endeavors.

Truth Has the Power To Unite and Connect

Allow me to share a few more words of wisdom from great thinkers of the past and present.

The German philosopher Immanuel Kant wrote, "Usually we do not come to know what forces [strengths] we have in the first place except by trying them out."[3] If we start with a negative attitude, we can never accomplish anything meaningful. We must boldly and courageously test our strengths and abilities. There are limitless spheres and areas in which we can do this.

Count Richard Coudenhove-Kalergi, the Austrian thinker and proponent of European unification with whom I met and talked on several occasions, wrote, "Truth unites and connects; it destroys the barriers that fallacies and lies have erected between human beings."[4] It is exactly as he says. Nothing is more powerful than truth; all lies and falsehood evaporate before it. Let's further consolidate our network dedicated to truth and justice.

Live Wisely!

President Toda was very strict with young people who dozed off during important or solemn occasions. He would shout: "You'll have plenty of time to sleep in your grave! Life is over in flash. What on earth are you doing?!"

Plato, the ancient Greek philosopher, said: "By nature, prolonged sleep does not suit either body or soul, nor does it help us to be active in all this kind of work [that is found in daily life]."[5]

Our lives are limited. It is a terrible loss to waste a single day, a single moment. Of course it's important to get enough sleep, and a balanced lifestyle with sufficient sleep is one of the foundations of good health. I hope that all of you will create value each day, living wisely and vigorously as you advance toward the great goal of *kosen-rufu*.

Beware of Ingratitude and Vanity

"Never become an ingrate!" This was one of Mr. Toda's injunctions.

The English playwright Shakespeare has one of his characters declare, "Ingratitude is monstrous."[6] Nothing is more fearful than ingratitude, both in the world at large and in the realm of Buddhism.

The French essayist and author Madame de Staël wrote, "Whatever belongs to vanity is of a transitory nature."[7] Nothing is more pitiful than those who are consumed by vanity. We have all seen people who rose to importance thanks to the sincere support of the Soka Gakkai only to forget that they owe everything to others. They become vain and proud, lose their faith and end up in the most wretched of circumstances.

Change Must Start With Human Beings Themselves

President Toda once remarked:

> The problems we see in government today also come down to the devilish functions inherent in life. They reside within the politicians who rule over government. The true nature of these devilish functions only becomes clear when we look at the Buddhist truth of the Ten Worlds existing within all people. In the same way, it is only possible to apprehend the devilish nature of political authority when we focus on the inner reality of human existence.

The devilish nature that resides in political authority originates from within human life itself. That is why the only way to truly change government at the deepest level is to bring about a fundamental transformation in human beings themselves.

The Heart of the First Three Presidents

The Scottish poet James Thomson wrote: "Let not brutish Vice of this [human frailty] avail, / And think to 'scape [escape] deserved punishment. / Justice were cruel weakly to relent."[8] Justice is strict—this is a point we must bear deeply in mind.

José Rizal, the great hero of Philippine independence, declared [with reference to a landmark book he had written about his people and his country's history], "I reply to all that has been written about us and to the insults they have heaped upon us."[9]

An unswerving commitment to fight against the enemies of Buddhism who seek to destroy *kosen-rufu* and the Soka Gakkai and to rigorously protect our members no matter what—this was the spirit of President Makiguchi and President Toda, and it is my spirit as well. Please know that this is the very heart of the Soka Gakkai's first three presidents.

From the August 7, 2004, Seikyo Shimbun

NOTES

1 Translated from Japanese. Lu Xun, *Rojin zenshu* (Collected Writings of Lu Xun), translated by Noboru Maruyama, et al. (Tokyo: Gakushu Kenkyu-sha, 1986), vol. 7, p. 521.
2 Translated from Japanese. Lu Xun, *Rojin zenshu* (Collected Writings of Lu Xun), translated by Toramaru Itoh, et al. (Tokyo: Gakushu Kenkyu-sha, 1986), vol. 10, p. 229.
3 Immanuel Kant, *Critique of Judgment*, translated by Werner S. Pluhar (Indianapolis: Hackett Publishing Company, 1987), p. 17.
4 Translated from German. Richard N. Coudenhove-Kalergi, *Ethik und hyperethik* (Leipzig: Neue Geist-Verlag, 1923), p. 48.
5 Plato, *The Laws*, translated by Trevor J. Saunders (London, Penguin Books, 1970), p. 297.
6 William Shakespeare,"Coriolanus," in *The Complete Works* (New York: Gramercy Books, 1975), Act II, Scene 3, p. 787.
7 Madame de Staël, *Reflections on Suicide* (New York, AMS Press Inc., 1975), p. 23.
8 James Thomson, *The Castle of Indolence*, edited by Alec M. Hardie (London: Hong Kong University Press, 1956), p. 41.
9 Carlos Quirino, *The Great Malayan: The Biography of Rizal* (Manila: Philippine Education Company, 1949), p. 110.

Advancing With the Same Mind As Nichiren Daishonin

AUGUST 2, 2004

As we aim toward the Soka Gakkai's eightieth anniversary in 2010, our members in every region of Japan are showing tremendous growth and moving ahead with vigorous momentum.

[*President Ikeda then went on to individually praise each of the thirteen regions around Japan for their efforts.*]

Recognize Negative Functions for What They Are

The Soka Gakkai's foundation is Nichiren Daishonin's writings. I'd like to begin my speech today with several passages from him.

First, in "Letter to Konichi-bo," Nichiren wrote, "Those who believe in the Lotus Sutra should beware of and guard themselves against the sutra's enemies" (WND-1, 664).

Faith is a struggle between the Buddha and devilish functions, between good and evil. Consequently, if we relax our guard even a little, devilish functions will quickly enter our lives. It is devilish functions that poison us with negative thoughts. That is why President Toda was always telling the leaders: "Keep out devilish functions! Dispatch them with the sharp sword of faith!"

In the same writing, Nichiren warned, "If you do not know your enemies, you will be deceived by them" (WND-1, 664).

The crucial thing is to be able to recognize devilish functions for what they are. That is what Buddhist study and faith are for.

During Nichiren's lifetime, there were individuals among his leading disciples—both priests and lay people who were respected by other followers—who became enemies of the correct teaching of Buddhism and brought pain and suffering to their fellow believers. We can see this same pattern in action today.

"The enemy exists within [the community of believers]," said Mr. Toda. "The 'worms within the lion's body' will try to destroy Buddhism," he strictly warned. He also said: "Beware of arrogant leaders and greedy priests. They'll end up betraying the Gakkai one day."

I have engraved these words in my heart, and they have proven to be correct down to the letter.

How base and immoral have been the actions of certain corrupt ex-members and of the priesthood in particular, which unilaterally cut off the Soka Gakkai that had done so much for it. You are all well aware of this.

In a letter of encouragement to followers [the Ikegami brothers] who were struggling amid persecution, Nichiren wrote: "From now on, too, no matter what may happen, you must not slacken in the least. You must raise your voice all the more and admonish [those who slander]" (WND-2, 597). We need to fight resolutely against the enemies of Buddhism even more strongly as Nichiren urged. If we don't, we will be unable to protect our precious organization dedicated to *kosen-rufu*.

Right up to the present, as President Toda's direct disciple, I have faced the firing line and taken on the full brunt of the innumerable attacks that have been directed at us. Throughout everything, never retreating a single step, I have protected the Soka Gakkai that Mr. Toda entrusted to me. I have prayed earnestly that our members would lead happy, healthy lives. It has been my greatest honor to do so.

Leave Behind an Immortal History

I would next like to cite a passage from "Questions and Answers about Embracing the Lotus Sutra."

Nichiren wrote, "When one has had the rare good fortune to be born a human being, and the further good fortune to encounter the teachings of Buddhism, how can one waste this opportunity?" (WND-1, 60). In this passage, Nichiren clarified the ultimate purpose of our existence. Our purpose or mission in this life is *kosen-rufu*; it is world peace and human revolution. Each of us, possessing our own precious mission for this lifetime, has become a member of the Soka Gakkai, the organization dedicated to fulfilling the Buddha's intent and decree. We are comrades in faith linked together by the deepest of bonds.

What a terrible waste it would be, therefore, if we were simply to float along in the organization built by our predecessors, without challenging ourselves or making any effort to advance our movement further. We should work with all our might to construct a towering monument of achievement in our lives and to boldly write a great history of struggle for the sake of *kosen-rufu*.

Let's create an immortal history that will leave a lasting impression on the lives of those who follow in our footsteps and will make them say, "I want to be like them!" Let's write an incredible history that will cause even our opponents to exclaim in admiration: "Excellent! Bravo!" That is the great way of life of Soka.

Faith Is the Foundation

Commenting on a passage from the Lotus Sutra, Nichiren wrote in "Conversation between a Sage and an Unenlightened Man":

> Even Shariputra [one of Shakyamuni's leading voice-hearer disciples], who was known for his great wisdom, was, with respect to the Lotus Sutra, able to gain entrance through faith and not through the power of his wisdom. How much more so, therefore, does this hold true with the other voice-hearers! (WND-1, 132)

Even Shariputra, known as "foremost in wisdom" among all Shakyamuni's disciples, only first grasped the mystic truth of the Lotus Sutra through faith. He attained enlightenment not through the power of wisdom but the power of faith.

Faith is the foundation of the Soka Gakkai. Those of strong faith—in other words, those who earnestly chant Nam-myoho-renge-kyo and dedicate themselves wholeheartedly to Gakkai activities—these are the people who are worthy of the highest respect. Such is the world of the Soka Gakkai.

Should the Gakkai ever develop into an organization that gives top priority to people's academic background or social status, it will have no future. It will no longer be the world of faith. I wish to emphasize this point very strongly.

Toda University

During the tumultuous times of postwar Japan, Mr. Toda's business fell into dire financial difficulty. Young as I was, I waged a lonely, solitary struggle to support his company.

One day, Mr. Toda said to me: "Daisaku, I'm sorry to have to ask this of you, but could you give up your studies? In return, I promise to give you a full university education myself."

From that time on, I visited Mr. Toda's home every Sunday, and he instructed me in every subject imaginable. Sometimes he would even invite me to stay for lunch or dinner. Mr. Toda possessed incredibly broad learning that encompassed politics, economics, law, Chinese literature, chemistry and physics. Later, Sundays weren't enough, so for several years he held classes for me in the morning before work. He poured his whole being into those classes, and I received his instruction with my whole being as well.

The intensive training I received at this "Toda University" made me the person I am today.

Advice to Young Women's Division Members

Mr. Toda frequently offered warm and compassionate advice to young women's division members. There is an episode in this connection that I incorporated in my novel *The Human Revolution*.

In September 1946, on his first regional propagation trip after the war's end, Mr. Toda offered this advice to two sincere sisters living in a mountain village in Tochigi Prefecture [which lies to the north of Tokyo and within the Kanto region]:

> Don't be in a hurry [to get married]. You'll be unhappy later on. . . . Practice with guts. You may think you've been cheated but keep practicing anyway. Put your heart into it. Whether you live in the mountains or in the city, you'll definitely find yourself the best possible husband. . . . It's your faith that's important, not where you live. Otherwise,

the Gohonzon would be false. . . . You have no cause to worry. None at all. With faith, you can change your destiny. I'll be keeping an eye on you. . . . Hold your head up. Don't belittle yourself. (*The Human Revolution*, book one, p. 167)

Mr. Toda wanted every young women's division member to become happy. Naturally, happiness is not found in marriage alone. Supreme happiness is found in a life of true and consistent faith.

At a young women's division meeting, Mr. Toda once said:

I want to see you all become happy. I want you to come to me in five or ten years and report to me, "Sensei, I have become so happy!" . . . You have many exemplary models in the women's division to look up to. They are examples of living happy, vibrant lives through sincerely chanting Nam-myoho-renge-kyo and having faith in the Gohonzon. I hope you will have the same faith in the Mystic Law and become happy, too.

Our young women's division members are showing wonderful development. The division's leaders are playing a pivotal role by setting fine examples, and many younger members are following in their footsteps. A steady stream of talented young women, each of whom has a tremendous mission, is being created. I am sure Mr. Toda would be delighted at this.

I hope all our young women's division members will triumph completely in the precious period of their youth and build a foundation for everlasting and indestructible happiness.

Cast Aside Vanity!

Italy, the birthplace of the Renaissance. It was in Italy, at the University of Bologna, one of the world's oldest universities, that I delivered a speech on the Renaissance genius Leonardo da Vinci and the United Nations, the "parliament of humanity" [in June 1994].

Da Vinci wrote in one of his famous notebooks, "The memory of benefits is a frail defense against ingratitude."[1]

The English poet John Milton wrote, "I could not omit [these words of high praise] without [incurring] a heavy charge of ingratitude."[2]

Gratitude is the path of humanity and the Buddhist way of life.

The ancient Greek philosopher Aristotle declared that wise people "will more than any other be happy."[3]

And he warned, "Vain people . . . are fools and ignorant of themselves."[4] These are words from more than 2,000 years ago, yet such people are still around today. The vain and conceited really don't know themselves. But others can see that they are just putting on an empty show that has nothing to do with reality.

When giving speeches or offering guidance as leaders, you mustn't think about making a good impression or showing people how clever you are. There's no need for that. The important thing is not to be a clever speaker but to offer reliable guidance in faith. Be energetic and sincere, and above all be yourselves. Speak the truth. Speak of your own experiences. Speak of Nichiren's writings. Speak of your personal conviction in faith. If you do that, you will naturally shine with humanity and draw others to you. I hope you will all strive to offer the kind of wonderful guidance that leaves people eager to hear more.

A Life Dedicated to Ideals

Words of truth can transform the times. I am reminded of the valiant French poet Victor Hugo, with his indomitable fortitude and love of the people.

Hugo once wrote to the champion of Italian independence Giuseppe Mazzini, calling out to the Italian people on the eve of their nation's unification: "Brothers. . . . Do not forget your fine and solemn Roman ideal. Be true to it. In that is your liberty, in that is your happiness."[5] These are stirring words.

I hope that all of you will also treasure your ties with your fellow members. If problems or difficulties are getting someone down, encourage them heartily. Remind them of their ideals, of their promise to carry out *kosen-rufu*, of their vow or their past dedicated commitment. The effort, the practice, to realize one's ideals is where true freedom and happiness are found.

Hugo also declared, "Material prosperity is not spiritual happiness."[6] There are so many people who are unhappy and miserable despite having material wealth and social recognition. True happiness lies in strength of spirit; it is found only in the midst of the struggle to carry out our unique mission in life.

Mr. Toda once said to me sternly: "Our lives are short, but what we achieve for *kosen-rufu* endures. Be a person who, in the short time allotted to him, joyfully writes through valiant actions a magnificent history that will live on forever, a history won through the workings of cause and effect." He also said, "No matter how innumerable the waves of malice and insult, never be defeated!"

I hope that all of you, people of profound mission, will inscribe your names in the golden annals of *kosen-rufu*. The crowning brilliance of the benefits that will adorn your lives as a result of your unceasing, dedicated efforts will shine on forever without fail to illuminate your descendents throughout future generations.

Congratulations on Your Victory!

The French writer and social activist Simone Weil urged the importance of transmitting the treasure of religion to youth and to the people: "Religious thought is genuine whenever it is universal in its appeal."[7] As we demonstrate the universality of the humanistic religion of Nichiren Buddhism, let us make even greater efforts to expand our movement for peace, culture and education around the world.

You are all outstanding leaders of *kosen-rufu*. Please live out your lives spearheading the way forward for countless members who follow behind you in the great struggle for world peace and the happiness of all humankind. Please adorn your noble lives with victory, celebrating and rejoicing in the Gakkai's victories and progress along the way.

Nichiren wrote:

Now, no matter what, strive in faith and be known as a votary of the Lotus Sutra, and remain my disciple for the rest of your life. If you are of the same mind as Nichiren, you must be a Bodhisattva of the Earth. (WND-1, 385)

Advancing with the same mind as Nichiren and with the conviction that you are Bodhisattvas of the Earth, please lead vigorous lives dedicated to *kosen-rufu*.

Stay well, and do your best as leaders of our great movement for *kosen-rufu*!

From the August 8, 2004, Seikyo Shimbun

NOTES

1 Leonardo da Vinci, *The Notebooks of Leonardo da Vinci,* compiled and edited by Jean Paul Richter (New York: Dover Publications, Inc., 1970), vol. 2, p. 297.

2 John Milton, *The Works of John Milton,* edited by Frank Allen Patterson, et al. (New York: Columbia University Press, 1933), vol. 8, p. 109.

3 Aristotle, *Nicomachean Ethics* (Bk. X: Ch. 8), in *Introduction to Aristotle,* edited by Richard McKeon (New York: The Modern Library, 1947), p. 537.

4 Ibid. (Bk. IV: Ch. 3), p. 388.

5 Translated from French. Victor Hugo, *Actes et Paroles,* vol. 2, *Pendant l'Exil, 1852–1870* (Paris: Albin Michel, 1938), pp. 134–35.

6 Translated from French. Victor Hugo, "Le droit et la loi," in *Oeuvres complètes* (Complete Works), edited by Jean Massin (Paris: Le Club Français du Livre, 1970), vol. 15, p. 597.

7 Simone Weil, *The Need for Roots,* translated by Arthur Wills (Boston: The Beacon Press, 1952), p. 93.

Initiate a Leadership Revolution

AUGUST 1, 2005

Thank you for attending our annual Nationwide Executive Conference!

The first half of this year—the year of the Soka Gakkai's seventy-fifth anniversary—has been marked by magnificent triumph, due to everyone's unified efforts based on the spirit of "many in body, one in mind." I would like to express my deepest gratitude to all of our members throughout Japan who are working so hard for *kosen-rufu*. Thank you very much!

Be Leaders Who Shine With Vitality

Leaders of *kosen-rufu* should shine with vitality. I hope all of you will rouse a dynamic and vibrant life force based on strong faith and encourage many people. I would like you to be leaders who can guide our precious members in the direction of happiness and victory. It is also crucial that you are able to keenly perceive the negative forces that seek to obstruct *kosen-rufu* and defeat them in their tracks, and that you speak out boldly for the truth. Your first priority as leaders is to state with courage what needs to be said in order to protect the Soka Gakkai, protect your fellow members and protect *kosen-rufu*.

I also hope you will make a concentrated effort to foster the youth who will shoulder the future. Young people need wings to enable them to soar freely. The wings that allow us to soar confidently into the future are none other than faith in the Mystic Law. Nichiren Buddhism is a teaching of unlimited self-improvement.

It is also essential that youth possess the sword of speech—namely, the ability to speak out for truth and justice—so that they can sever the roots of all lies and slander that inflict pain and suffering on people.

Toward that end, I hope that the senior leaders of our organization will always give foremost thought to how they can make it easy for the youth to carry out their activities and allow them to give full play to their talents and potential. I have high expectations for you in this regard.

Second Soka Gakkai president Josei Toda said: "A disciple has to follow the path of a disciple. Both in word and deed, we have to manifest our mentor's teaching in our lives." The mentor-disciple spirit is the very core of the Soka Gakkai. We have always advanced with that spirit; we have always won through the oneness of mentor and disciple. Please never forget this essential point.

A building will collapse if its main pillar is toppled. In the same way, if the Soka Gakkai loses its central pillar—the spirit of mentor and disciple—it, too, is bound to perish.

True Gratitude for a Mentor's Compassion

Mr. Toda's manner was always extremely solemn when he spoke of his memories of his mentor, first Soka Gakkai president Tsunesaburo Makiguchi. When he talked about the latter's death, in particular, tears would fill his eyes and he would get very worked up.

Mr. Makiguchi was arrested by the militarist authorities during World War II for his efforts to protect the integrity of Nichiren Buddhism. One after another, his other disciples deserted him to save themselves. In a display of appalling ingratitude, some of them even cursed him as they departed. Only Mr. Toda remained loyal to his mentor and steadfast in his faith. Later, he expressed his gratitude to Mr. Makiguchi, saying, "In your vast and boundless compassion, you let me accompany you even to prison." This is the spirit of mentor and disciple in Buddhism. Mr. Makiguchi and Mr. Toda were connected at the deepest level of existence.

Mr. Makiguchi stayed true to his convictions and died a heroic death in prison. Mr. Toda left prison alive and, with an indomitable determination equal to that of the Count of Monte Cristo, set out to vindicate his mentor. He began his struggle to fundamentally reform a society that would persecute a good, honest person.

At the ceremony [in 1949] marking the sixth memorial [fifth anniversary] of Mr. Makiguchi's death, Mr. Toda remarked:

> After I got out of prison, I learned for the first time that President Makiguchi's funeral had been conducted by a few relatives and a mere two or three others who were not frightened away by the watchful eyes of the authorities. Hearing the kind of funeral that had been held for this great man who produced the *Theory of Value,* my blood boiled with indignation, and I vowed to myself with a passionate determination, "I will make my mentor's name known throughout the world."

I have lived my life in the same spirit, and I have made the great achievements of Presidents Makiguchi and Toda widely known.

Triumphant Dawn of Mentor and Disciple

Mr. Toda also said, "I am prepared to dedicate the rest of my life to proving whether my mentor's actions were right or wrong." On another occasion, he declared, "My determination to carry on after my mentor and to fight until I have ensured that the Gakkai's mission in the world is fulfilled remains absolutely unchanged."

I, in turn, served my mentor, Mr. Toda, with complete devotion. When his business fell into a state of crisis after the war and many of his employees deserted him, I alone stood up to support him. My vow as a disciple whose spirit was one with his was to protect him no matter what, even at the cost of my life. I did not receive a salary for months on end, and I didn't even have an overcoat to get through the winter. I was so tired every night that I sometimes didn't have the energy to take off my shoes before I collapsed in my room.

How earnestly I fought! How many hardships I experienced and endured!

But through this united struggle of mentor and disciple, the situation started to improve, and a faint ray of light began to glimmer at the end of the tunnel. And, on May 3, 1951, having surmounted all obstacles, Mr. Toda was finally inaugurated as the second president of the Soka Gakkai. It was a triumphant dawn realized through the victory of mentor and disciple. From this point, the Soka Gakkai began its remarkable advance, eventually growing into the global organization it is today.

Leadership Positions Mean Responsibility

"A fish rots from the head," goes an old saying. When the top leaders of an organization become corrupt, the entire body begins to rot and eventually collapses. This is a universal truth. Furthermore, when leaders become arrogant and cease listening to others' opinions, devilish influences take hold. That's why Mr. Toda sternly said to leaders: "The higher your position, the greater your responsibility. You need to be a model to others." He also warned, "You may profess grand sentiments publicly, but if you don't actually put them into practice in your own life, you are the worst kind of leader."

On yet another occasion, he remarked, "When a company's executive comes to work late and the employees also give in to laziness and start arriving late for work on a regular basis, problems are bound to arise and the business will decline." Mr. Toda was very strict about how one starts off the morning.

Produce a Fresh Momentum

Mr. Toda also said, "No one will follow your lead if you don't exhibit the courage to fight for what's right." Leaders must exert themselves wholeheartedly on the front lines. You mustn't become leaders who sit back and rely on the strength of the organization without making any personal effort.

Everyone thought that the Osaka campaign of 1956 was a lost cause, but I went myself to the front lines of the struggle and refused to let our small numbers defeat us, ultimately achieving a momentous victory. Together, my beloved fellow Kansai members and I made the impossible possible.

When leaders stand in the vanguard and personally take action, everyone else can advance with confidence. It is important for leaders to produce a fresh momentum. They need to take the initiative in talking to others about Buddhism, introducing people to our Buddhist practice, studying Nichiren's writings and encouraging members wholeheartedly so that they can stand up and take action, too. Let us all work together to carry out such a leadership revolution.

Everything Is Determined by Our Heart

Mr. Toda also said:

> There are three kinds of people in the Gakkai. The first are those who appreciate and support the Gakkai, which is striving to achieve *kosen-rufu*. The second are those who are just following along in the organization, neither causing trouble nor contributing anything positive to the movement. Finally, there are those of ill intent who seek some sort of compensation from the Gakkai, thinking that the organization owes them something for all they have done. This last group is the one that causes the most problems.

Everything is determined by our heart, our inner attitude or spirit. As Nichiren stated, "It is the heart that is important" (WND-1, 1000).

If we're going to practice Nichiren Buddhism, we should do it with a pure heart and spirit, so that people around us will be inspired and invigorated by our presence. In the same vein, I hope the youth will set a wonderful example based on faith that draws the admiration and praise of others.

The age of youth is here. I call on our young people to step forward and assume full responsibility for our movement. At the same time, it is tradition in the Soka Gakkai for our men's and women's division members to also advance with the dynamism of youth. The Gakkai spirit shines in such vitality.

Remain young at heart as long as you live! Keep pressing forward with a sparkle in your eyes! That is the realm of faith and the way of life of human revolution.

From the August 3, 2005, Seikyo Shimbun

Promoting a Culture of Peace

AUGUST 1, 2005

In May of this year, the first class of students graduated from Soka University of America in Aliso Viejo, California. They are truly to be commended for their diligent efforts. Despite SUA being a newly established school, more than thirty of its graduates were accepted into postgraduate programs at top universities in the United States and around the world. This fact has prompted astonishment and praise from leading figures in many fields.

Some SUA graduates have begun the next phase of their lives by joining the workforce in their native countries. Others are making a new start with the United States as their place of mission. The members of the first graduating class are great pioneers who brought their profound passion and ideals to this brand new school. They are all precious, talented young people with a noble mission. I sincerely hope and pray that each will lead a life of victory and success.

The Inspiring Development of the SGI-USA

The SGI-USA continues to make remarkable strides under the leadership of General Director Danny Nagashima. In the past five years, the SGI-USA organization has grown from 1,600 districts to nearly 2,500. This year, in particular, has witnessed a splendid expansion of the *kosen-rufu* movement. This is wonderful! Congratulations!

In September 2005, the SGI-USA and SGI Canada cooperated in successfully holding the first North American Study Conference. At present, plans are being considered for a North and South American Study Conference to be held at the Florida Nature and Culture Center in the United States with the participation of representatives from Canada and Brazil.

Coupled with a rise in immigration, the United States is becoming an increasingly multilingual country. Recognizing this trend, the SGI-USA has held study conferences and cultural events in several languages. They are also working on further developing the National Language Bureau, which supports activity groups that use languages other than English. The SGI-USA's weekly newspaper, *World Tribune,* is already publishing issues in nine languages: English, Spanish, Chinese, French, Korean, Portuguese, Thai, Cambodian and Japanese. These steps have been taken based on a desire to respond to the needs of members of various linguistic and cultural backgrounds so that they may conduct joyful and hope-filled activities.

Additionally, the SGI-USA has been conducting activities in support of the United Nations, including the Building a Culture of Peace for the Children of the World exhibition at venues across the United States. The SGI-USA intends to promote more of these types of programs, in line with requests from UN representatives.

A Culture of Peace Resource Center has been established at both the SGI Plaza in Santa Monica, California [SGI-USA Headquarters], and the SGI-USA New York Culture Center. These resource centers offer publications and information on UN-related activities and feature the Culture of Peace exhibition on permanent display.

In June 2005, the Committee of Religious Nongovernmental Organizations at the United Nations appointed Hiro Sakurai of the SGI's UN Liaison Office in New York to serve as its president. Mr. Sakurai is an alumnus of the Soka University of America graduate school.

The RNGO comprises representatives from 110 UN-accredited nongovernmental organizations that define their work as religious, spiritual or ethical in nature, including groups that are grounded in Christian, Islamic and Buddhist traditions. The selection of an SGI representative as committee president can be viewed as a sign of the trust that these various NGOs from around the world place in our organization.

Let's offer another round of applause in praise of our friends in America for their efforts to gain wider understanding and trust for our movement in society!

When the Young Women's Division Shines, the Gakkai's Future Is Bright

Second Soka Gakkai president Josei Toda held profound hopes for the activities of the members of the young women's division. I completely share these feelings. The potential of young women is truly immense. When a young woman upholding the Mystic Law seriously sets herself to the task, she can bring about a major transformation of the destiny of her family and can also change her community for the better. Like a shining sun of hope, she can impart courage to everyone around her.

The cheerful, courteous behavior and sincere, pure-hearted efforts of our young women's division members move the hearts of many others. They have the capacity to make allies of various kinds of people.

When the young women's division members shine, the Gakkai's future is bright; on the other hand, if they don't develop, the Gakkai's future will be dark. In order to build a strong foundation for the next fifty years, now is the time to focus our efforts on fostering young women's division members. Let's give our all toward revolutionizing the young women's division.

At meetings of the Kayo-kai, a young women's division training group, President Toda gave guidance on various matters by quoting from Nichiren's writings and the classic works of world literature. On one occasion, he referred to the novel *Little Lord Fauntleroy* by Frances Hodgson Burnett.

Little Lord Fauntleroy tells the story of Cedric, an American boy. After his father's death, little Cedric is sent to England to live with his grandfather, a member of the aristocracy. The ill-tempered grandfather's heart is gradually opened by the influence of Cedric's innate goodness and sincerity. Mr. Toda commented: "Cedric's complete trust in his grandfather heals the crusty old man's heart and transforms the entire situation. An unwavering belief can profoundly influence everything. Young women's division members should be like this."

Mr. Toda also said: "Women need to study and cultivate themselves. Please live life with a heart that is always rich. Advance in high spirits with a charm that is vibrant and refreshing."

Speaking with Kayo-kai members on another occasion, Mr. Toda cited a passage from Nichiren's writing "On the Four Stages of Faith and the Five Stages of Practice": "They [my disciples] are like an infant emperor wrapped in swaddling clothes, or a great dragon who has just been born. Do not despise them! Do not look on them with contempt!" (WND-1, 789). Mr. Toda added:

We who uphold the Gohonzon embody the properties of the Buddha of the Mystic Law. As such, we are fundamentally different from those who harbor and spread erroneous teachings. We are honored to share the same life-state as the Daishonin. We should be proud of this and lead victorious lives with a noble and lofty spirit. We mustn't disparage ourselves.

You possess the greatest philosophy in the world. Each of you has an important mission. That is why you mustn't put yourselves down or belittle yourselves. Please do not get caught up in shallow ways of living that go against your inherent worth.

Mr. Toda wanted all young women's division members to find true happiness. And I feel exactly the same way.

Move Forward With an Expansive and Open Spirit

To all our leaders, I ask that you be sure to recognize and value those who are working behind the scenes. Please become fine leaders of shining character who are admired for inspiring confidence and peace of mind in those around them.

Of course, it is not enough to merely be good-natured. It is necessary to be strict about matters regarding faith. We must fight resolutely against anyone or anything that threatens to harm the Gakkai. Remember, "The voice carries out the work of the Buddha" (OTT, 4). The way to protect the Gakkai is to speak out boldly with words of truth. I hope our youth division members in particular will take the lead in these endeavors. When I was a young man, I fought with everything I had under Mr. Toda. I never let the arrogant get away with maligning the Gakkai or despising the common people.

It's not about appearances. Those who are concerned about impressing others or making themselves look good cannot wage a wholehearted struggle. Whether it is in expanding our movement, introducing Buddhism to others or fostering capable people, we need to achieve clear, tangible results. This is the struggle of genuine disciples and a challenge befitting youth.

It is especially important for those who have been appointed to new positions in our organization to set fresh goals for growth and advance toward them. These goals should give everyone hope and motivation; they should never make members feel burdened. Please move forward with an expansive and open spirit.

Nichiren said: "My wish is that all my disciples make a great vow" (WND-1, 1003), and "The 'great vow' refers to the propagation of the Lotus Sutra" (OTT, 82). Worldwide *kosen-rufu* is the direct path to peace. Let's live our lives to the fullest as we strive toward this grand ideal.

From the August 4, 2005, Seikyo Shimbun

None Are More Noble Than Those Who Strive Wholeheartedly for *Kosen-rufu*

AUGUST 2, 2005

Growth and expansion are the traditions of the Soka Gakkai's youth division. I was a youth division member, too. In the early days of our movement, I served as a young men's division corps chief. We all strove eagerly, competing to increase the membership in our respective corps and foster new people. Our young hearts were filled with the dream of *kosen-rufu*, a glorious, hopefilled vision of the future. We brimmed with fighting spirit. The energy and exuberance of the youth division inspired and galvanized the Gakkai as a whole. The men's division, women's division and youth division were joined in a wonderful spirit of solidarity. The Soka Gakkai's history is one of the youth opening new doors in our movement for *kosen-rufu* through their dynamic efforts to win without fail. This has always been, and must always remain, the spirit of the youth division.

A Commitment to Achievement

President Toda frequently stressed that men should strive to cultivate ability. I want you, our young men's division leaders, to step forward and take on big challenges. Please strive in a free and dynamic manner.

People who are appointed to important leadership positions but lose courage and vision cannot achieve great things. It's a shame to spend one's life passively, just doing the minimum to get by, never taking any personal initiative. Since we are part of the great struggle for *kosen-rufu*, let's achieve results of which we can be proud! Let's create a record of actual proof for all to see! This is the spirit of the Soka Gakkai young men's division.

It All Comes Down to Us

Kosen-rufu is a struggle to foster capable people, shape a bright future and create world peace. Those who have wholeheartedly dedicated themselves to this noble cause enjoy boundless and immeasurable benefits in lifetime after lifetime. We cannot savor "the greatest of all joys" (OTT, 212) through halfhearted efforts or empty posturing and pretense. It all comes down to us. We ourselves are the ones who decide everything.

Nichiren Daishonin wrote, "The Law does not spread by itself: because people propagate it, both people and the Law are respectworthy" (GZ, 856). Let us together lead truly worthwhile lives propagating the supreme Law. Everything we do for *kosen-rufu* benefits us as well as our family and fellow members. This is irrefutable in light of Nichiren's writings and the sutras.

How has the Gakkai achieved the momentous victories it has? It is solely due to the earnest struggles of the women's and young women's divisions. I wish to express my most profound gratitude to all Soka women, who are like shining suns of humankind. Thank you!

As I have stressed repeatedly, it is vital that our organization values women and listens to their ideas and opinions. I wish to reconfirm this point once again today. Male leaders need to respect, appreciate and praise our women's and young women's division members, who are striving with immense dedication. As long as the men in our organization have that spirit, the future of *kosen-rufu* will be bright and expansive.

To enable the young women's division, which has such a great mission, to strengthen its unity and advance with even greater momentum, I ask that all our members, especially those of the women's division, support and encourage them.

Should there be male leaders who discriminate against women or arrogantly order them about, I ask that you sternly take them to task, for such behavior cannot be tolerated in our organization.

Protect Those Who Are Working Hard for Kosen-rufu

The aim of the Soka Gakkai is *kosen-rufu*. As such, those working with all their might to realize that goal are supremely noble and admirable. As an organization, we must value them above all. The members don't exist for the sake of the organization; the organization exists only for the sake of the members. Of course, our organization is important, but any leaders who exploit it and behave arrogantly because of their position have got their priorities completely reversed. We must strictly reprimand anyone who is guilty of such conduct.

The role of leaders is to protect and support the members striving for *kosen-rufu*.

Equality Between Men and Women

A position of authority doesn't make a person important, and there's no justification for looking down on ordinary people. Everyone is equal. This naturally means that men and women are equal. In a resounding declaration of gender equality, Nichiren wrote:

> There should be no discrimination among those who propagate the five characters of Myoho-renge-kyo in the Latter Day of the Law, be they men or women. Were they not Bodhisattvas of the Earth, they could not chant the daimoku. (WND-1, 385)

This is the fundamental spirit of Buddhism.

Today, I'd like to briefly note examples of the humanism that prevailed in Shakyamuni's community of believers.

Shakyamuni lauded exemplary disciples irrespective of their gender. In a Buddhist text known as the *Anguttara-nikaya* (Book of Gradual Sayings), he lists the names of several outstanding female disciples and describes their strong points, praising them respectively for their unexcelled wisdom, proficiency in the rules of discipline, skill in teaching the dharma (Law), meditative powers and so on.[1] Shakyamuni highly commended women who dedicated themselves selflessly for the sake of the Law and the happiness of others.

Safety Reminders

In Shakyamuni's community of believers, there were also highly detailed regulations regarding travel by female disciples—that is, by nuns of the Buddhist Order. For example, one sutra touches on the perils that befell women traveling alone in those times. Concerned for their safety, Shakyamuni set forth rules of training that proscribed them from going out to villages, crossing rivers or staying away for a night alone, unaccompanied by another nun.[2] These practical guidelines were designed to prevent harm coming to his female disciples.

It's important for us, too, to remind one another to be careful and on the alert. A well-timed word can thwart devilish functions.

Leaders of the women's and young women's divisions, please make "safety" and "no accidents" top priorities in all your activities.

The Buddhist canon also records female disciples' expressions of gratitude to Shakyamuni. One of them declared, "I indeed, revering the enlightened one [the Buddha], best of men, am completely released from all pains, doing the teacher's teaching."[3] This passage clearly conveys the joy of striving in Buddhist practice under Shakyamuni's instruction, of surmounting karma and approaching life with a fresh, revitalized spirit.

Seeking spirit and steadfast practice are the keys to growth and victory; they are also sources of inspiration, peace of mind and development.

With an Open Heart!

In one of her poems, the American poet Emily Dickinson wrote that losing one's faith surpasses the loss of an estate.[4] How true this is. Dickinson ranks alongside Walt Whitman as one of the nineteenth century's preeminent poets.

I often share the words of great writers and thinkers throughout history in my essays and speeches. Learning from their spirit provides the opportunity to gain an even deeper understanding of Buddhism. I also share their words because I believe that they help communicate our message to those who don't practice our faith. In his writings, Nichiren, too, quoted from many different works, including Buddhist scriptures, Chinese and Japanese classics and legends and fables to express the essence of Buddhism. The Daishonin was broad-minded and open to the world, and so is the Gakkai.

The Standard Operating Procedure of Devilish Functions

I'd now like to share several passages from Nichiren's writings with you.

First, in "The Workings of Brahma and Shakra," he observed:

> Those possessed by a great devil will, once they succeed in persuading a believer to recant, use that person as a means for making many others abandon their faith. (WND-1, 800)

This is the standard operating procedure of devilish functions—trying to persuade one person to abandon faith and then using that person to lead many others from the correct path.

Nichiren further wrote:

> Some people, despite their shallow understanding, pretend staunch faith and speak contemptuously to their fellow believers, thus often disrupting the faith of others. (WND-1, 800)

We must rigorously condemn the grave offense of disrupting the harmonious body of believers. Our denouncing wrongdoing and teaching the correct path are also in the best interest of those who commit such offenses. It is vital that we thoroughly rebuke and deal stringently with wrongdoing in the organization, so that our juniors will not repeat the same errors. That's true compassion.

In the past, we have seen leaders and influential figures in our ranks who, led astray by ambition and self-interest, abandoned their faith, betrayed their fellow members and tried to destroy the Soka Gakkai. As you know, all of them have met the most ignominious ends. The Buddhist law of cause and effect is very strict indeed.

An Alliance of the Good-hearted

In one of his writings, Nichiren cited a passage relating to "evil friends"[5] from a commentary by the Great Teacher Chang-an, explaining:

> Evil friends employ enticing words, deception and flattery, clever speech and an affable manner, and in this way cause others to do evil. And in leading them to do evil, they are destroying the good minds that are in them. (WND-2, 220–21)

Keep evil friends at arm's length. With strong faith, see through them and repudiate their actions. Members of the youth division, I'm counting on you. I hope you will continue to expand and strengthen our alliance of good-hearted friends!

From the August 5, 2005, Seikyo Shimbun

NOTES

1 *The Book of the Gradual Sayings (Anguttara-nikaya), or More-Numbered Suttas,* translated by F. L. Woodward (Oxford: Pali Text Society, 1995), vol. 1 (Ones, Twos, Threes), p. 21.

2 *The Book of the Discipline (Vinaya-Pitaka),* translated by I. B. Horner (Oxford: Pali Text Society, 1993), vol. 3 (Suttavibhanga), pp. 186–90.

3 *The Elders' Verses II: Therigatha,* translated by K. R. Norman (Oxford: Pali Text Society, 1995), p. 17.

4 Emily Dickinson, *The Complete Poems of Emily Dickinson* (Boston: Little, Brown, and Company, 1960), p. 180.

5 Evil friends: Also, evil companion or evil teacher. One who causes others to fall into the evil paths by misleading them in connection with Buddhism. An evil friend deludes others with false teachings in order to obstruct their correct Buddhist practice.

Seek Out Training That Will Make Your Life Shine

AUGUST 2, 2005

I am sure you are all familiar with the renowned German poet Friedrich von Schiller. I was an avid reader of Schiller's works in my youth, and I memorized many of his poems. My mentor, Josei Toda, being aware of that, once suddenly demanded, "Please recite one of Schiller's poems for me." Mr. Toda was constantly testing and training me in one form or another. He was a very strict mentor and a man of great learning.

Strict Training in Youth

I was the editor-in-chief of *Boys' Adventure*, a magazine published by one of Mr. Toda's companies. Later, it was renamed *Boys' Japan*, and I worked hard to improve the content. I had frequent opportunities to talk with authors, whom I would go out to meet in order to arrange for them to contribute articles to the magazine. Because I was eager to produce the best possible children's magazine, my discussions with these writers often became rather passionate and drawn out.

After finishing an appointment, I'd rush back to the office, only to find Mr. Toda glaring at his watch with obvious impatience. "You're late!" he'd bark out. "Were you dawdling around?" Another time, when I returned to the office after picking up a manuscript from a writer, Mr. Toda asked me to describe the content for him. His question put me on the spot. I'd been so intent on bringing back the manuscript on time that I hadn't had a chance to read it. His query made me break out in a cold sweat.

Mr. Toda was incredibly exacting. He could even be intimidating. Sometimes I found his strictness painful and harrowing to endure. Yet above all, I experienced great joy in striving alongside my mentor. It was a pleasure to struggle together with him.

For me, those were days of intense training. Mr. Toda fully understood that, in order to foster outstanding character, it is necessary to provide strict training. The education I received from him was thorough in all respects. I am truly grateful for Mr. Toda's excellent instruction. I am what I am today due to the training that I underwent in my youth, and I am very proud of this.

Of course, the times have changed since then. Still, it is most wonderful to receive guidance and to polish oneself within the supremely humane world of the Soka Gakkai. Precisely because we live in more fortunate times, I hope young people in particular will actively seek out training.

Leaders bear a heavy responsibility; the growth of an organization depends upon the growth of its leaders. Therefore, I hope all leaders will make a profound determination and launch a great advance that will create a history of fresh victories.

"Worms Born of the Lion's Body"

I'd like to share some passages from the writings of Nichiren Daishonin.

In the letter "Encouragement to a Sick Person," Nichiren wrote:

> It is the way of the great devil to assume the form of a venerable monk or to take possession of one's father, mother, or brother in order to obstruct happiness in one's next life. Whatever they may say, however cleverly they may try to deceive you into discarding the Lotus Sutra, do not assent to it. (WND-1, 81)

Devilish functions may enter into the lives of those who appear as venerable monks or the lives of one's parents or siblings in an attempt to cause one to discard faith in the Lotus Sutra. This is a pattern we can still observe today. These destructive functions use insidious means to hinder one's attainment of Buddhahood. We should never be deceived by anyone who presses us to give up our faith or our commitment to *kosen-rufu*. One cannot expect to gain benefit by leaving the Soka Gakkai—which is propagating the Mystic Law—and losing one's pure faith. This will only send one tumbling down the path of misfortune. You are all well aware of this, having seen others travel this course.

Though brief, this passage from the Daishonin contains an important warning. Mr. Toda also used to refer to it often.

In another writing, "Letter from Sado," Nichiren stated:

> Neither non-Buddhists nor the enemies of Buddhism can destroy the correct teaching of the Thus Come One, but the Buddha's disciples definitely can. As a sutra says, only worms born of the lion's body feed on the lion. A person of great fortune will never be ruined by enemies, but may be ruined by those who are close. (WND-1, 302)

Here, Nichiren strictly warned that Buddhism is not destroyed by external enemies but from within. This deserves careful consideration.

In "Letter to the Brothers," Nichiren further wrote:

> Believers in the Lotus Sutra should fear those who attempt to obstruct their practice more than they fear bandits, burglars, night raiders, tigers, wolves, or lions—even more than invasion now by the Mongols. (WND-1, 495)

Those who obstruct the advance of the Soka Gakkai—an organization carrying out the Buddha's will and decree—and inflict suffering on its members are far worse than any fearsome bandit. That is why it is vital that we fight resolutely against such enemies and denounce their malevolent schemes. For every word of false criticism, hit back with ten—no, a hundred—words of truth. It is important to speak out with righteous indignation and thoroughly refute their lies. More than anyone else, leaders need to be serious about this point, or they will be defeated by devilish influences.

Never Compromise With Evil

Let's examine a few more passages from Nichiren's writings. In "The Votary of the Lotus Sutra Will Meet Persecution," he advised his disciples, "In this defiled age, you should always talk together and never cease to pray for your next life" (WND-1, 449). And in "Letter from Teradomari," he wrote, "Those resolved to seek the way should gather and listen to the contents of this letter" (WND-1, 206). Both of these letters were written in the midst of harsh persecution. Unity and mutual encouragement are most important. Our efforts to gather in friendly harmony to study Nichiren's writings and learn the spirit of *kosen-rufu* are in complete accord with the Daishonin's teachings.

Nichiren frequently warns of the destructive influences of what Buddhism terms "evil friends."[1] In the writing "What It Means to Slander the Law," he cited this famous passage from the Nirvana Sutra: "Even if you are killed by a mad elephant, you will not fall into the three evil paths [of hell, hunger and animality]. But if you are killed by an evil friend, you are certain to fall into them" (WND-2, 258). He then commented: "If one cares about the next life, one should fear all kinds of causes that lead to rebirth in the evil paths. But even more than such causes, one should fear evil friends or teachers" (WND-2, 258).

In "On Reciting the Daimoku of the Lotus Sutra," Nichiren noted, "In bringing about the ruin of the nation and causing others to fall into the evil paths, there is nothing to surpass the harm done by evil friends" (WND-2, 222). There are unscrupulous individuals who, while appearing to be good, are driven by ambition and self-interest and try to exploit the Gakkai. Don't be deceived by such scoundrels.

Buddhism is strict. By compromising with evil, one is bound to follow wrongdoers down the path to misfortune and suffering. Therefore, the Daishonin teaches us to staunchly battle against evil that threatens to destroy Buddhism.

The Global Soka People's Movement

My dialogue with the British historian Arnold J. Toynbee is one of my life's unforgettable memories. Dr. Toynbee remarked that we are in need of a world religion that can open people's eyes, awakening everyone to the fact that we all belong to the human family and that our species is a part of the life of the entire universe. Also, in an article he contributed to a Japanese magazine, he wrote that religion endows limitless potential on humanity.

Dr. Toynbee had a special interest in Buddhism, a quintessential philosophy from the East. He was intrigued by the Soka Gakkai's efforts to actualize the teachings of Buddhism in the modern age. That is what led him to write me, requesting that we engage in a dialogue. At the time, it was difficult for him to travel to Japan, mainly due to his advanced age. And that's why I accepted his invitation to visit him in London.

Dr. Toynbee and his wife kindly welcomed me to their home. Though he was a world-class scholar, Dr. Toynbee was completely free of arrogance or self-importance. I was young enough to be his son, and he treated me with utmost warmth and sincerity. He was a great scholar. During our dialogue, he said to me:

> The present threat to mankind's survival can be removed only by a revolutionary change of heart in individual human beings. This change of heart must be inspired by religion in order to generate the willpower needed for putting arduous new ideals into practice.[2]

The broad-based people's movement of the Soka Gakkai that drew Dr. Toynbee's attention and expectations has now become a huge groundswell encompassing the world. Leading thinkers around the globe are praising it as a source of hope for humanity. With deep pride, let us advance along the great path of Buddhist humanism, the great path of happiness.

From the August 6, 2005, Seikyo Shimbun

NOTES

1 Evil friends: Also, evil companion or evil teacher. One who causes others to fall into the evil paths by misleading them in connection with Buddhism. An evil friend deludes others with false teachings in order to obstruct their correct Buddhist practice.

2 Arnold Toynbee and Daisaku Ikeda, *Choose Life: A Dialogue*, edited by Richard L. Gage (New York: Oxford University Press, 1989), p. 63.

Faith Is the Ultimate Courage

Dedicating our lives to truth and justice, we have nothing to fear. This is the spirit of those who practice Nichiren Buddhism. If we are to protect our noble fellow members, we mustn't be cowardly. As leaders, we must forge ahead intrepidly, always striving with all our might on the front lines of *kosen-rufu*.

In my struggles as a member of the youth division, I often encountered individuals who denigrated President Toda and repeatedly directed groundless criticisms at the Soka Gakkai. I couldn't bear to let such injustices go unchallenged, so I went around personally to talk with those people to set the record straight. By clearly proclaiming the truth about my mentor and presenting the rightness of the Gakkai's actions, I often succeeded in winning them over on the spot and turning them into supporters and allies.

Mr. Toda taught that we should proceed with confidence and boldness. If the members of the Soka Gakkai are cowardly and fainthearted, unable to take action and fight at a crucial moment, then no matter how great their numbers, *kosen-rufu* will never move forward. As Nichiren wrote, "The mighty sword of the Lotus Sutra must be wielded by one courageous in faith" (WND-1, 412). Although we may possess the unrivalled sword of the Mystic Law, it will be impossible for us to defeat devilish functions with it if we are cowardly.

Courage is a hallmark of youth. Therefore, youth, please have courage! Faith is the highest form of courage. People of true courage always stand alone. I am proud of the fact that I shouldered complete responsibility for the Soka Gakkai from a young age. I was thirty-two when I became the third president.

The three obstacles and four devils always arise on the road to *kosen-rufu*. My life has been a nonstop battle against devilish forces bent on destroying Nichiren Buddhism. My mind is never at rest 365 days a year; I am thinking unceasingly of the welfare of my fellow members in Japan and around the world. That is the honest truth.

The presence of negative forces spurs us to battle against them, and it is through our efforts to challenge ourselves in that struggle that we grow and develop and come to savor profound joy in the depths of our lives—a joy that we share with our fellow members who strive wholeheartedly alongside us. There is no greater pride and honor in life than this.

Buddhism Is Winning

How do we open the way forward? By personally taking action as leaders and showing concrete results in our struggles for *kosen-rufu*. How do we win people's trust and understanding? By demonstrating our sincerity and integrity, meeting directly with people, treating them with courtesy and respect and listening to what they have to say. This is the only way.

Everything begins with our attitude and our efforts as leaders. It's not up to others. It's up to us.

If all that leaders do is assign the hard work to others while trying to avoid making any effort themselves, then we have no need for them. Leaders who behave this way will only erase all their past good fortune, and the organization as a whole will stagnate.

Buddhism is a struggle to be victorious. It is win or lose. What decides the outcome is the attitude or commitment of leaders. They must strive in the vanguard and brim with fighting spirit. Leaders who always exude energy, vitality and joy, leaders whose lives shine, will be victorious.

The Power of One Woman

As I have said repeatedly, I hope you will all value and respect the young women's division. Mr. Toda often stressed this point as well. From my youth division days on, I have always placed great importance on the opinions of young women. This was my mentor's advice. If the young women's division grows and develops, the Soka Gakkai's future will be assured. That is because one vibrant young woman can exhibit the power of ten or a hundred people.

There are countless examples at workplaces around Japan, for instance, where the efforts of a single young women's division member have had a powerful effect in promoting trust and understanding of the Soka Gakkai throughout her entire company or organization.

Young women also play a central role in their families. Very few fathers dare to disobey their daughters' commands! [Laughter] When a young woman marries, she leads her husband, and if she has children, she shoulders a large part of the responsibility to raise them as successors of our movement.

The members of the young women's division have a huge mission. Their range of activity is infinite. Above all, it is my wish that they enjoy happiness, and the time for them to build the foundation for that happiness is in their youth. I also hope they will be women who possess strong, pure-hearted faith.

I'd like our male leaders to always treat our young women respectfully and chivalrously. Those places where women can freely and vibrantly demonstrate their abilities to the fullest are bright, happy, refreshing and have limitless potential for growth. Those places that value women flourish and triumph in the end.

Working for the People's Welfare

I'd like to share comments from leading thinkers about the importance of political leaders' dedication to the welfare of the people.

The renowned American economist Professor John Kenneth Galbraith remarked in the course of our dialogue [which was serialized in the Soka Gakkai-affiliated magazine *Ushio* from August 2003 through June 2004]: "I was able to meet a number of politicians through working for [various] political administrations. I can level a certain antipathy to politicians who are not concerned with the people at large and are concerned with their own aspirations or their own doctrines. Reforming this is a core requirement of a good political scene." One should be highly critical of politicians who claim to be interested in the welfare of the majority when in fact their agenda is completely self-centered.

He also said, with regard to the qualities he looked for in political leaders: "I want politicians who identify themselves with the people at large and not the fortunate few. That is the great division in all modern politics, and I want them to be on the side of the numbers, not the few who are fortunate." All too often, we have witnessed lawmakers behaving pompously while looking down on the people. It is crucial that we see through such hypocrisy.

On the subject of women's equality, Dr. Galbraith commented, "I don't see any division in common sense and good politics as between men and women." And he added, "Our society must strive to eradicate discrimination against women in all aspects." I entirely agree. A society that fails to heed women's opinions is destined to decline. This situation needs to be an important focus of governments from now on.

Gratitude to All Living Things

Nagarjuna, the great Mahayana scholar of ancient India, wrote in a work addressed to a king, "In whatever sphere it may be, please always do whatever you can to help the people."[1] He also left these words: "You should strive to benefit others with no thought of recompense. Shoulder all hardships alone, and share all joys with others."

In a similar vein, King Ashoka had the following edict carved on one of his famous stone monuments: "All my efforts are an attempt to fulfill the debt I owe to all sentient beings."[2] Political leaders should feel a profound gratitude to all living things that support their existence and repay that debt of gratitude through their actions. This, I feel, must be the essential spirit of all who are involved in government.

In our dialogue, Chile's former president Patricio Aylwin remarked, "I believe that religions, in that they promote the spiritual uplift of humanity and engender the values of moral improvement and understanding, solidarity and peace among human beings, contribute decisively to elevating the quality of politics."[3]

Dr. Margarita Vorobyova-Desyatovskaya of the Institute of Oriental Studies of the Russian Academy of Sciences, a world-renowned scholar of the Lotus Sutra, expressed the view that it would be ideal if political leaders possessed religious faith out of a desire for spiritual self-improvement, adding that this would pave the way toward governments that work for the people and with the people.

Creating New Value in Local Communities

Dr. Vincent Harding, professor at the University of Denver and friend of the late Dr. Martin Luther King Jr., has a high opinion of the Soka Gakkai's social activism, saying that both Gandhi and King believed the true purpose of faith was to promote social activism and create new value. The Soka Gakkai, too, he notes, is actively engaged in local communities and society as a whole, working from a foundation of social justice and compassion. As an organization that manifests its beliefs in concrete action, it is a movement with which all can sympathize and support, he said.

The world is watching the vigorous advance of our great humanistic movement. Let's continue to advance boldly toward victory with ever-growing momentum.

From the August 7, 2005, Seikyo Shimbun

NOTES

1 Translated from Japanese. Nagarjuna, *Hogyo osho ron* (The Precious Garland of Advice to a King), in *Daijo Butten: Ryuju ronshu* (Mahayana Buddhist Texts: The Writings of Nagarjuna), translated by Ryushin Uryuzu (Tokyo: Chuo Koronsha, 2004), vol. 14, p. 276.

2 Translated from Japanese. Keisho Tsukamoto, *Ashoka-o hibun* (King Ashoka's Stone Edicts) (Tokyo: Daisanbunmei-sha, 1976), pp. 92–93.

3 Translated from Spanish. Daisaku Ikeda and Patricio Aylwin, *Alborada del Pacifico* (Dawn of the Pacific) (Santiago, Chile: Centro de Acción Internacional, Centro de Estudios, Universidad Miguel de Cervantes, 2002), p. 58.

Each Person Has a Unique Mission

AUGUST 4, 2005

True champions are those who rise to the challenge at a crucial moment. Times of great trial are actually opportunities to acquire vast, everlasting good fortune. Nothing comes of being daunted or discouraged. First and foremost, it is important to chant. When we do so, the way forward opens up before us, and we will definitely gain happiness. Consider each challenge as an opportunity to chant Nam-myoho-renge-kyo. It is all for our own benefit.

While being sure to take care of your health, summon forth an overflowing life force and laugh away your troubles. Enjoy them. The more imposing your problems seem, the stronger and more positive you should strive to be! Move forward with a light heart, singing a song of hope. People gladly gather around those who are cheerful and optimistic, no matter what happens. Places where people have this spirit are sure to triumph and flourish.

Fostering Capable People Through Wisdom and Prayer

Today, there are SGI members in 190 countries and territories around the world. [As of the publication of this book, the number has grown to 192.] This remarkable development has been possible because we have valued and cherished each individual. It has come about as a result of wholeheartedly encouraging each person and facing struggles together with courage. In this way, we have cheerfully enacted a drama of victory on the stage of society and life.

Each person has a precious and irreplaceable mission. As the Buddhist teaching of cherry, peach, plum and damson blossoms indicates, each person may be considered a special, distinct flower. It is the power of the Mystic Law that enables each of us to bring our potential to full bloom and to fulfill our unique mission. Each individual is a capable person in his or her own way; each person has a valuable purpose. That is why it is crucial for us to foster and support new members with all our hearts.

As Nichiren stated: "To accept is easy; to continue is difficult. But Buddhahood lies in continuing faith" (wND-1, 471). It is vital that we remain steadfast in faith throughout our lives. That is the way to forge a life-state of eternally indestructible happiness. For this reason, I would like seniors in faith to provide members with personal guidance and encouragement in faith. This is a shining tradition of the Gakkai and a source of its strength. Guidance is a form of fostering people. Its purpose is to enable people to develop their capacity to further *kosen-rufu*.

It is also necessary to learn about faith through one's practice and activities for *kosen-rufu*. The Soka Gakkai organization itself can be likened to an academy of philosophy or a university for developing capable people. Areas throughout Japan have a splendid heritage of fostering talented individuals. Some exemplary regions have, over the course of nearly three decades, created a great river of tens of thousands of capable people who have studied the history of the Soka Gakkai and the spirit of mentor and disciple.

Wisdom arises from strong commitment and determination. Wholehearted, earnest prayer is essential.

Rather than employing one set format across the entire nation, I'd like to see each region bring forth its own creativity and ingenuity and develop its own methods for creating fresh waves of capable people.

A Shining Rainbow of Friendship in Mongolia

I have received a report from a delegation of Soka Gakkai representatives who are visiting Mongolia. Yesterday [Aug. 3, 2005], they paid a courtesy call on former Mongolian president Natsagiin Bagabandi at the government offices in Ulaanbaatar, the capital. In May 1998, during his tenure as president, Mr. Bagabandi visited Soka University where he delivered an address. I met with him on that occasion.

[In his recent meeting with the Soka Gakkai delegation, Mr. Bagabandi offered congratulations to President Ikeda on having been awarded the Order of the Pole Star, one of Mongolia's top national honors. The former head of state also expressed appreciation for Mr. Ikeda's efforts to promote friendship between Mongolia and Japan.]

The Soka Gakkai delegation also met with Dr. Dojoogiin Tsedev, a noted Mongolian writer and rector of the Mongolian University of Arts and Culture. Dr. Tsedev and I are currently engaged in a dialogue that is being serialized in the Soka Gakkai–affiliated monthly magazine *Pumpkin*.

[Speaking with the Soka Gakkai representatives, Dr. Tsedev mentioned that newly elected Mongolian president Nambaryn Enkhbayar voiced his hope that the SGI president would visit Mongolia. Mr. Ikeda has met with President Enkhbayar on three occasions and forged cordial ties.]

In 1275, following the first Mongol invasion of Japan, the military government in Kamakura wantonly executed the five Mongol envoys who had been sent to Japan. Nichiren lamented, "It is indeed a pity that . . . the innocent Mongol envoys have been beheaded" (WND-1, 628). He wished for the happiness of all humanity, transcending differences in nationality or ethnicity.

Now, more than seven centuries later, the Soka Gakkai [which espouses Nichiren Buddhism] is contributing significantly toward promoting amicable relations between Mongolia and Japan. Mongolia's political and cultural leaders are extending immense trust and appreciation to our organization. This would no doubt delight the Daishonin.

[Mr. Ikeda has also received honorary doctorates from six Mongolian universities in recognition of his contributions to friendship between the two nations. In addition, as a symbol of peace and friendship between Mongolia and Japan, an Ikeda Peace Park has been established in Mongolia's Dornod Province, the scene of the Battle of Nomonhan, in which an alliance of Russian and Mongolian troops fought against Japanese forces in 1939.]

The Integrity To Reject Wrongdoing

Our progress contributes to establishing the humanistic principles of Buddhism in society and creating an ever-widening sphere of peace and happiness.

Shakyamuni was once asked by a disciple to explain how many kinds of ascetics [monks and nuns] there were. The Buddha replied that there were four.[1] Among these was "one who defiles the way," of which Shakyamuni offered this description: "Making [only] a semblance of those with good vows, insolent, defiler of families, reckless, deceitful, unrestrained, [mere] chaff, going in disguise, one is a defiler of the way."[2] Here, he is talking about those who, though having renounced secular life to seek the way, are arrogant and scheming. The priests of Nichiren Shoshu [led by Nikken] are a typical example of this. You must never allow yourselves to be fooled by those who act important and pretend to be wise but are base and corrupt within.

President Toda was very fond of the Chinese classic *Compendium of Eighteen Histories*, and I also studied it under his tutelage. In it, Liu Pang [also known as Emperor Kao-tsu], the founder of the Han dynasty, was told by a retainer on the eve of battle: "Those who practice virtue will prosper, and those who go against virtue will perish. A battle launched for no good cause cannot be won. Therefore, if we can make clear the wrongs of our opponent, victory is certain to be ours." What wrongs are being committed by one's opponent? What is the purpose for struggling against them? This passage argues that victory goes to the side that is clear on these points.

The *Compendium of Eighteen Histories* also records the words of Shih Le, who established the Later Chao dynasty in the fourth century CE: "The great man must handle all matters in an open, fair, and honest manner, as clear as the light of the sun and moon." When leaders are honest and fair, possessing an integrity that will not accept any corruption or evil, people will trust and follow them.

Transforming One's Community Into an Oasis of Hope

Exactly twenty years have passed since the tragic crash of a Japan Airlines jumbo jet [the worst accident in Japanese aviation history].

[On Aug. 12, 1985, Japan Airlines flight 123 traveling from Tokyo to Osaka crashed into the side of Mount Osutaka in Ueno Village, Gunma Prefecture, killing 520 passengers and crew members. There were only four survivors.]

My wife and I offered solemn prayers in memory of the victims. It was a terrible tragedy, and I still remember the day that it happened most vividly. As I briefly mentioned last year, among the local rescue workers who rushed to the scene were two Soka Gakkai members—Kenji Saito and Akinori Izumi, now both vice chapter leaders. At the time, Mr. Saito was a young men's division greater block leader [the equivalent of today's young men's division district leader], and Mr. Izumi was a men's division district leader. Both have been actively contributing to the welfare of their communities.

How admirable it is to be deeply rooted in one's community and exert oneself for the sake of others. Steadily carrying out such activities builds trust and understanding and becomes the driving force to transform one's community into an oasis of vibrant hope. I have only the highest praise for members who strive unceasingly to serve their communities.

Requirement for Leaders in the Twenty-first Century

Nichiren wrote, "Thus within the tents of command they were able to devise strategies that assured victory a thousand miles away" (WND-2, 391). It is important to devise the best possible strategy. Consensus and coordination are crucial in this respect. Then, based on that, decisive action opens the way to victory. I hope you will exercise brilliant and inspiring leadership with all the power and sensitivity of a symphony composed by Beethoven.

Our struggles for *kosen-rufu* can be very challenging. But to the degree that we exert ourselves for others' happiness and in spreading Nichiren Buddhism, we can gain immense benefit. In lifetime after lifetime, we will be reborn as great leaders who enjoy a state of supreme happiness. Our activities enable us to accumulate causes that will make this possible.

I call on our youth division members to act dynamically and freely in their various places of mission. Newly appointed leaders in particular must take care not to let their positions go to their heads. Taking on the hard work oneself rather than leaving it for others—never forget that this is a requirement for leaders in the twenty-first century.

From the August 9, 2005, Seikyo Shimbun

NOTES

1 Four kinds of ascetics: They are (1) one who knows the way, (2) one who teaches the way, (3) one who lives the way, and (4) one who defiles the way.
2 *The Group of Discourses (Sutta-Nipāta),* translated by K. R. Norman (Oxford: Pali Text Society, 1995), vol. 2, p. 11.

Live With Passion,
Live Without Regrets

AUGUST 4, 2005

This autumn [on Nov. 18, 2005], the Soka Gakkai will celebrate its seventy-fifth anniversary. We are undergoing a mighty, historic struggle. Let's press forward boldly, with dignity and confidence—for our own sakes, for society and for our eternal happiness throughout the three existences.

As the weather is very hot now, please watch out for your health.

Nichiren Daishonin wrote, "You will grow younger, and your good fortune will accumulate" (WND-1, 464). People of strong faith brim with youth and vitality. If we strive earnestly to spread Nichiren Buddhism, we will become vigorous and healthy.

Our second Soka Gakkai president, Josei Toda, would be quite strict with us, stating that if we lacked a sparkle in our eyes and a healthy glow, dignity and compelling charm, we couldn't truly be practicing faith. If anyone wearing a sluggish, unfocused expression approached him, he'd bark out: "What's the matter with you? Stop looking so defeated!"

Buddhism is not about high-sounding words; it is found closer to home, in the little things. Let's make each day one of victory, living energetically and free of regret.

Mr. Toda once said: "Those in charge should arrive to work as early as possible. By doing so, the employees will feel a deeper sense of responsibility and will work their hardest. This will set the course for victory in the struggles that work entails." When I worked at Mr. Toda's company, I was always the first to arrive at the office. I spent my days doing everything I could to support my mentor, striving with all my might for *kosen-rufu*.

"Always in the vanguard!" That was my spirit and pride as a youth.

The dynamic energy of youth propels great undertakings; it is the force that makes the Soka Gakkai strong. I call on you, our youth, to show actual proof in your respective workplaces and local organizations, so that you can proudly declare, "I have won!"

Maintain the Basics of Your Faith

Regarding corrupt individuals who stirred up trouble for the Soka Gakkai, Mr. Toda would say indignantly, "People with rotten characters are always causing problems." It is vital that we staunchly oppose heinous behavior. We must use all our wisdom and combat it with everything we have.

Mr. Toda also remarked, "My life is precious to me, but those striving earnestly for *kosen-rufu*, those working so hard in our organization dedicated to *kosen-rufu*, are the most important of all." I completely agree with his sentiments. If leaders in particular make an even greater effort to value and care for their fellow members, the Soka Gakkai is certain to grow and develop further.

Mr. Toda was very strict with those who held high positions in the organization. "Nothing is more pitiful than a leader who has forgotten the basics of faith," he said. Also, "People may appear very capable, but if they lack the basics of faith, their faith will crumble in a moment." The basics of faith, of course, are none other than faith, practice and study. I hope all of you will conscientiously maintain these basics and become leaders worthy of the trust and respect of all.

Eradicating Evil Allows Good To Emerge

During the time of our first president, Tsunesaburo Makiguchi, almost all of the Soka Gakkai's top leaders caved in to persecution by the militarist authorities and quit the organization. Following the war, Mr. Toda stood up alone to rebuild the Soka Gakkai. Even then there were those who feared persecution and cowardly renounced their faith.

In the course of advancing *kosen-rufu*, it is only natural that the three obstacles and four devils will appear.

We must especially be on guard against individuals who, having once embraced the correct teaching of Buddhism, betray their faith and seek to destroy the harmonious community of believers, our pure realm of mentor and disciple and of unified purpose.

Soka Gakkai members are generous and trusting. The Soka Gakkai is a gathering of warmhearted, friendly people. But we mustn't be deceived by ill-intentioned individuals or permit the unity of our *kosen-rufu* movement to be disrupted. If we neglect the fight to eradicate evil, good cannot emerge. This is a fundamental principle of Nichiren Buddhism.

In the Soka Gakkai, the highest praise belongs to those who actually struggle to realize *kosen-rufu*.

Protect the Community of Believers

The Buddhist sutras forbid actions that would destroy the community of believers. Allow me to share a few of those warnings with you now.

As membership in the early Buddhist Order grew, there appeared an increasing number of practitioners who, succumbing to laziness, arrogance or envy, committed various offenses and tried to cover them up. A certain disciple described this situation: "Although devoid of virtuous qualities, running affairs in the Order the incompetent, the garrulous, and those without learning will be strong. Although possessing virtuous qualities, running affairs in the Order in the proper manner, the modest and unconcerned will be weak."

Further, there were lazy and corrupt practitioners who disregarded the mentor's words. [A sutra states, "Those fools, being thus (un)trained, without respect for one another, will take no notice of their preceptors, as a bad horse takes no notice of the charioteer."]

Practitioners who sought to disrupt the harmony of the Buddhist Order and, though warned, refused to abandon their efforts were severely punished as were their supporters and cohorts. They had to confess their offense in front of the entire Order and vow never to repeat it. In some cases, offenders were even expelled from the Order.

One sutra states that those who disrupt the harmonious community of believers are destined to suffer in hell for an entire *kalpa*. In other words, they would fall into a state of endless torment.

When the traitor Devadatta attempted to divide Shakyamuni's community of believers, those who aided and abetted him were severely reprimanded as "contributors to schism" and "accomplices in destroying the harmony of the Buddhist Order."

Furthermore, monks who transgressed the rules of discipline were forbidden to participate in full gatherings of the Order. Among those falling under this ban were those who had disrupted the harmonious community of believers or who had schemed to do so. If a monk tried to conceal such an offense and attend a gathering anyway, the other monks had a right to prevent him from doing so. If a precept-violating monk was found to have gained entry to a gathering, anything that had been decided during those proceedings was rendered invalid.

We Are an Assembly of People Whose Speech Promotes Harmony

Shakyamuni was especially strict about the offense of duplicity, or speaking with a forked tongue. This is also known as "alienating speech," because when fallacious words are spread about, they can drive wedges between people and encourage divisiveness, discord and conflict.

Shakyamuni described a person who uses such speech as a "slanderer" who "sows discord among those who were in harmony or foments those who are at variance." "Discord," he continued, "is his pleasure, his delight, his joy, the motive of his speech." He rebukes monks guilty of such behavior, asking why they are so foolhardy as to promote friction.

The realm of Soka is a gathering of children of the Buddha, a united force for good. It is an assembly of people whose speech promotes harmony. We must never allow our organization to be damaged by attempts to cause division.

Among Nichiren's disciples was a priest called Sammi-bo who, though he was extremely learned, abandoned his faith. In a letter describing Sammi-bo's unfortunate end, Nichiren wrote, "I mention it so that others can use it as their mirror" (WND-1, 998).

In other words, he recorded the tale of Sammi-bo's fate as a lesson for future generations.

The history of our movement is rigorously documented, as is our struggle for truth and justice against corruption and error. Based on earnest prayer, mutual support and encouragement, let us ensure that the Soka Gakkai forever advances as a harmonious community of believers.

Impart Sound Values and the Spirit of Truth and Justice

This August [2005], Soka University of America, Aliso Viejo will welcome its fifth entering class [the Class of 2009]. Bright students from around the globe, brimming with passion and enthusiasm, will gather for the new academic year. As the university's founder, nothing makes me happier.

SUA opened in May 2001. Plans to expand and enhance the university's facilities toward its tenth anniversary are now under discussion. Let's give our full support to the establishment of this institution of higher learning, which is dedicated to educating leaders of peace.

In Japan, the birth rate is plummeting and the population aging rapidly. Universities and also many other organizations and institutions are battling desperately to survive. To do so, they are devoting their energies to fostering capable young people. In our case, the future division members [those members in elementary, junior high and high school] are precious treasures who will shoulder the

Soka Gakkai's future and carry on the cause of world peace. They all have a noble mission.

When it comes to raising children, warm humanity and inspiring character are qualities needed not only by teachers in particular but also adults in general. Teachers, it has been said, should be their students' servants. In the coming years, the quality of teachers and their dedication to their students will become increasingly important. Adults need to grow as human beings first. We should keep this point in mind.

Please commend these young people's efforts, point out their better qualities and further spur their growth by praising and encouraging them. Impart to them sound values and the spirit of truth and justice. Sometimes playing the comedian to make them laugh, at other times speaking as a wise philosopher, share with them your strongest convictions.

Please become people who are greatly trusted and respected by the youth.

I still remember the wonderful teachers I had in elementary school. Children never forget the kindness of adults. The encouragement they receive in childhood stays with them as treasured memories throughout their lives.

Deep, honest communication is most important. Please ignite the flame of high ideals in their young hearts. Now is the time to train and foster our youthful successors.

From the August 10, 2005, Seikyo Shimbun

Index (Volumes 1 and 2)

ability, men and 2: 85

abuse, target of 1: 28

academics 2: 64

action 1: 36, 91, 2: 19; decisive 2: 112

activities, benefits of doing, for *kosen-rufu* 1: 2, 2: 112–13; consequences of separating from 1: 37. *See also* Soka Gakkai activities

advancement, creating fresh, 66; Daisaku Ikeda's spirit for 2: 36; human characteristics for 1: 41–42; spirit for 2: 38, 48–49, 51, 94, 106, 115; unending 2: 46

actual proof, record of 2: 86

adeptness, testing 2: 56

adults, qualities for 2: 121

adversaries 2: 56; Josei Toda's warning about 1: 56

adversity 1: 85

Aeschylus, on traitors 1: 51

Africa, *kosen-rufu* movement in 2: 41

"age of conflict," in the Latter Day of the Law 1: 56

Age of Soka 1: 3

Akiya, Einosuke 1: 123; Nichiren Shoshu priesthood, dismissal by 1: 124; Nikken's behavior toward 1: 124

Alain 2: 33

"alienating speech," power of 2: 119

Amiel, Henri-Frédéric, "Doing good requires courage" 1: 60; "The enervated are unfortunate" 1: 60

anguish 1: 3

Anguttara-nikaya (Book of Gradual Sayings) 2: 88

Anhui University 1: 107

Anzai, Shin, priesthood's attack on the Soka Gakkai, comment on 1: 130

apathy 1: 20

appearances 2: 84

appreciation 1: 116

Archias, Aulus Licinius 1: 80;
Cicero's defense of 1: 81
Aramaki, Tetsuro, priesthood's
attack on the Soka Gakkai,
comment on 1: 130
Arendt, Hannah 2: 23
Aristotle 2: 5, 8, 44, 67
arrogance 1: 67 2: 5; form of 1: 19;
guarding against 2: 57; Josei
Toda on 2: 12, 25; and leaders
2: 56
Asahi University 1: 130
Ashoka, on gratitude 2: 105
attitude, arrogant 1: 2; benefits
of maintaining pure 1: 10;
inner 2: 39, 76; negative
2: 56; Nichiren Daishonin
highlighting importance of
2: 76
authority, position of 2: 87;
secular 1: 50
Aylwin, Patricio 2: 105

Ba Jin, quotes of truth and justice
by 1: 135–36
backslide, never 2: 39
Bagabandi, Natsagiin, Daisaku
Ikeda, appreciating 2: 109
beauty, true 1: 10
behind the scenes, recognizing
people working 2: 83
Beijing University 1: 107, 2: 55
beliefs, Nichiren Daishonin
describing people of
steadfast 1: 98; steadfast
1: 74
belittle, Josei Toda describing
reason not to 2: 83

benefits, basis for gaining
immense 2: 112; scope of 2: 26
Bergson, Henri-Louis 1: 11
Bharat Soka Gakkai [SGI-India]
1: 44
Bibesco, Marthe 1: 102
The Big Question: How Philosophy
Can Change Your Life
(Marinoff), Daisaku Ikeda
quoted in 1: 106; study of
Nichiren Daishonin in 1: 106
birth rate, positive view of the
decline in 2: 40
Bodhisattva of the Earth,
Nichiren Daishonin outlines
the spirit of 2: 69
Boston Research Center 1: 3, 105;
impact of the works published
by 2: 52
brand-new, spirit of always
starting 1: 86
Brecht, Bertolt 1: 116
Buck, Pearl 1: 107
Buddhahood, attaining 1: 110, 2:
64; path of attaining 2: 26
Buddhas 2: 24; becoming 1: 99;
behavior of 1: 19; Josei Toda
outlining way to become
1:134–35; Nichiren Daishonin
outlining criteria for attaining
2: 108; noble work of 2: 31;
obstacles to attaining 2: 95;
will of 1: 120
Buddhism 2: 97; battle in 2:
13; cause for destroying
2: 96; consequence of not
admonishing the enemies
of 2: 62; essence of, 36;

fundamental spirit of 2: 88; life of 1: 38; Nichiren Daishonin defining outcome of practicing 1: 88; Nichiren Daishonin stating lifeblood of 1: 50; Nichiren Daishonin's warning about internal enemies of 2: 95; number eight in 2: 37; power of 1: 7; practicing 1: 8; principle of 1: 31, 60; purpose of 2: 12–13; struggle in 2: 103; teaching of 1: 13, 38, 60, 2: 22, 45, 115; true 2: 33; way of 2: 51

Buddhism: Introducing the Buddhist Experience (Mitchell) 1: 105

Buddhist, model of a true 2: 24

Buddhist compassion, Josei Toda describes 2: 25

Buddhist members, effect of meeting 1: 18; respecting 1: 12

Buddhist Order, action against individuals disrupting the unity of 2: 118–19; action against precept-violating priests in early, 2: 119; instances of corrupt practitioners in early 2: 118–19

Burnett, Frances Hodgson 2: 82

Caribbean, and SGI members 2: 26

caring, Josei Toda's emphasis on 2: 15

Carson, Rachel 1: 86

cause and effect, Buddhist law of 1: 12, 2: 25, 91

censure, Tsunesaburo Makiguchi on 1: 62

Chang-an 2: 91

Ch'angho 1:137

challenge 1: 109; Buddhist handling 2: 107

champ, true 2: 107

character, 2: 83; cultivating outstanding 1: 31, 2: 94; developing 1: 37; education and 1: 13

Chartier, Emile. *See* Alain

cheerful 2: 107

Chihaya (mountain fortress) 1: 108

children, and encouragement 2: 121; and kindness 2: 121; lasting memories in 2: 121; qualities needed for raising 2: 121; raising 1: 62

Chuko K'ung-ming 1: 54, 56, 65, 2: 38; Daisaku Ikeda's impression of philosophy of leadership of 1: 68; evaluating character, methods of 1: 72–73; stating attributes of superior leader 1: 69

Churchill, Winston 1: 102

Cicero, Marcus Tullius 1: 77–78, 83; and Buddhism 1: 51; European culture, influence on 1: 77–78; evil and corruption, weapon against 1: 79; on friendship 1: 80

Columbia University 2: 52

commitment 2: 108

community, basis for transforming 2: 112;

foundation for building trust
in 1: 93
companies, criteria for growth
and prosperity of 1: 45
compassion 1: 19; Josei Toda's
substitution for 1: 60;
lack of, 41; Nichiren
Daishonin's expression of 1:
13; true 2: 90
competion, Winston Langley's
views of overcoming negative
1:4
confidence 2: 48; inspiring 2: 83
consensus 2: 112
conviction, person of 1: 13
Constitution, Japan: article 9 of
1: 4
cooperation 1: 61
coordination 2: 112
correct teaching, seeking 2: 43
Coudenhove-Kalergi, Richard
2: 56
courage 1: 102, 109, 2: 101;
gaining true 1: 45; igniting 2:
49; Josei Toda on 1: 60, 2: 75;
lionhearted 1:137; Nichiren
Daishonin states the person
of 1: 14; personal 1: 78; power
of 1: 102
courtesy, exercising 2: 102
cowards, Tsunesaburo Makiguchi
on 2: 55; Tsunesaburo
Makiguchi describing 1: 23
Cuba, and SGI members 2: 26

Daibyakurenge, 1991 issue of 1:
124
Daisaku Ikeda research groups,

establishment of 1: 106–07, 2:
54–55. *See also* Soka humanism
deceit 1: 44
dedication, serious 2: 31
defeat, cause of 1: 41, 60; Josei
Toda stating cause for 1: 1;
path to 1: 20
Deng Xiaoping 2: 53
Dengyo 1: 14, 2: 23; The
Regulations for Students of
the Mountain School 2: 43
descendants, efforts that will
bring benefits to 2: 68–69
destruction, path to 1: 34
determination 1: 137, 2: 108;
benefits of having a strong 1:
11; firm 1: 118
Devadatta, modern-day 1:
126 (*See also* Nikken);
reprimanding the action of 2:
118–19
devilish functions, defeating
2: 89; effect on leaders
influenced by 2: 91; Josei
Toda highlighting existence
of 2: 62; Josei Toda stating
effect of being defeated by 2:
13; Josei Toda's warning to
guard against 2: 61; Nichiren
Daishonin describing pattern
of path of 2: 95; Nichiren
Daishonin stating workings
of 2: 90; Nichiren Daishonin's
warning to recognize 2: 61–62;
quality needed to defeat 2:
101–02
development, sources of
2: 89

devils, Nichiren Daishonin on
2: 46
dialogue 2: 102; one-to-one 1:
17–19, 42
Dickinson, Emily, on faith 2: 89
difficulties, encouraging
members experiencing 2: 68
disasters, Nichiren Daishonin
stating cause of 1: 36
disciples, struggle of genuine 2:
84
discussion meetings, leaders and
1: 20
disunity, warning against
attempts of, in the Soka
Gakkai 2: 119
Djourova, Axinia D., *The Beauty of
a Lion's Heart* 1:111
Doshisha Women's College of
Liberal Arts 1:131
dozing, Josei Toda's strictness
about 2: 57
On Duty (Cicero), 77–78

École Normal Supérieure
(university) 2: 33
education, higher 2: 22
efforts, incremental 1: 41–42; not
making 2: 26
elderly, Buddhist view of helping
2: 40
Eliot, T.S., death 2: 20; *The Four
Quartets* 2: 20; *Notes Toward the
Definition of Culture* 2: 20; *The
Waste Land* 2: 20
Emerson, Ralph Waldo, call 2:
7; describing duty of human
being 1: 96

encouragement 2: 120; Nichiren
Daishonin outlining
importance of mutual 2: 96
source of 1: 78
"Encouraging Devotion" chapter
(Lotus Sutra) 1: 120
end result, deciding 2: 103
On Ends (Cicero) 1: 78
enemy, greatest 1: 85
energy 2: 103
Enkhbayar, Nambaryn, hopes of
2: 109
envy 1: 31
equality 1: 95; gender 2: 105;
Nichiren Daishonin's
declaration of gender 2: 88
error, speaking out against 2: 30
Europe, *kosen-rufu* movement in
2: 41
European unification, exponent
of 2: 56
evil, action against 2: 97;
consequence of not fighting
2: 117; and corruption 1: 79;
effect of negotiating with 2: 97
"evil friends," Nichiren
Daishonin describing
workings of 2: 91; Nichiren
Daishonin warning
destructive influences
of 2: 97
evil, accomplices to 1: 30;
Nichiren Daishonin's spirit
to combat 1: 36; source of
1: 50; source of all 1: 20;
Tsunesaburo Makiguchi's
conviction of denouncing 1: 30
existence, Nichiren Daishonin

clarifying purpose of
practitioners 2: 63
expansion 2: 85
experiences, faith 2: 67

Fables (La Fontaine) 1: 97
factions 2: 48; Josei Toda against
forming 1: 70
failure, cause of 1: 81–82
fainthearted, consequences
of being 2: 101–02; effects
of being 2: 101; Josei Toda
declaring about being 2: 12
faith 1: 21 2: 8, 48, 95, 117, 2: 101;
academic qualifications and
1: 10; basis of 2: 117; benefit
of exerting in 1: 109; benefit
of strong 2: 91; and courage
1: 46; and daily life 1: 112;
effects of discarding 1: 62;
guarding against individuals
abandoning 2: 117; Josei Toda
on 1: 61, 2: 65–66; learning
about 2: 108; lifeblood of 2:
29; money and 1: 10; Nichiren
Daishonin describing
conditions under people
abandoning 1: 98–99; Nichiren
Daishonin discussing spirit
of 1: 110; Nichiren Daishonin
emphasizing 1: 61; Nichiren
Daishonin's encouragement
to never discard, 102;
organizational position and
1: 13; person of genuine 1:
13, 101; power of 1: 14, 2: 64,
137; prime point in 1: 109;
pure-hearted 2: 104; purpose

of 2: 12–13, 62; root of 1: 99;
scope of 2: 77; societal status
and 1: 13; and society 1: 112;
spirit of 1: 23, 109; steadfast 1:
13, 2: 108; strong 1: 88, 2: 104;
struggle of 2: 61
"faith equaling excellent health"
1: 10
"faith manifesting itself in daily
life" 1: 10
falsehoods 1: 80; importance of
exposing 1: 44
family, and faith 2: 22–23; young
women's role in 2: 103
fear, Josei Toda on 1: 41
fearfulness, and defeat 1: 46;
Tsunesaburo Makiguchi on
1: 50
first North American Study
Conference 2: 80
La Fontaine, Jean de 1: 97
forward, moving 2: 40; way for
leaders to open way 2: 102
fostering 2: 5, 86
"Fostering youth," Josei Toda's
emphasis on 2: 13
freedom, finding true 2: 68
friends 1: 80
friendships, benefit of fantastic 2:
5; forming 2: 21; forming true
1: 75
Furuta, Takehiko, and Japanese
militarism 1: 5
future, creating a triumphant
1:137; key to a bright 2: 45;
Nichiren Daishonin describing
facets for creating victorious
1:137

Future Division Dynamic Growth
Month 2: 21
future division leaders,
appreciating 2: 22
future division members,
fostering 2: 120–21; hopes
for 2: 22; noble mission of 2:
120–21

Gakkai spirit, true 2: 6
Galbraith, John Kenneth 1:
87; discrimination against
women, views about 2:105;
qualities for politicians,
highlighting 2: 104; *Toward
Creating a Great Age of
Humanism* 2: 21
Gandhi, Mahatma, on ahimsa
[non-violence] 1: 44–45; on
unity 1: 44
Gaulle, Charles de, spirit 2: 48–49
General Lodging Temples,
completing constructing of 1:
121–22
Germany 2: 23
Ghana 1: 61
goals 2: 51; defining 1: 59;
Josei Toda's encouraging
youth division about 1: 78;
maintaining 1: 74–75, 78;
setting clear 2: 84
Goethe, Johann Wolfgang von
2: 6
Gohonzon, attitude between
members in front of 1: 95;
benefit of practicing to,
mirrors the words of the Lotus
Sutra 2: 12–13

good, cause for manifesting 2:
117; championing 2: 6; doing
1: 60; erasing leaders' 2: 103;
force for 1: 115; highest 2:
6; Tsunesaburo Makiguchi
deploring people of minor 1:
51; Tsunesaburo Makiguchi
highlighting factors working
against people of great 1: 62;
Tsunesaburo Makiguchi's
describing people of minor
1: 36
good fortune, acquiring 1: 49, 2:
51, 107; enjoying 1: 36
Gohonzon, benefits of practicing
to, resonating with words
of the Lotus Sutra 2: 12–13;
relations between members in
front of 1: 95
Gorbachev, Mikhail 1: 88
Gorbachev, Raisa 1: 88; gratitude
to Soka Gakkai member,
expressing 1: 89; Kansai
Soka schools, thoughts at 1:
90; Soka Gakkai members,
impression of 1: 89; women
and peace, comments on 1: 89
governments, focus of 2: 105;
Josei Toda outlining true way
to change 2: 58
Gorbachevs, works of 1: 89–90
Grand Main Temple [Sho-Hondo]
1: 122
Grand Reception Hall
[Daikyakuden] 1: 122
gratitude 2: 67
great vow, in Nichiren Buddhism
2: 84

"the greatest of all joy," enjoying 2: 86
greatness, obstacle of 1: 79; people of 1: 38
growth 2: 85; catalyst for 1: 99; experiencing personal 1: 31; key to limitless 2: 3; keys to 1: 137, 2: 89
Guangdong Academy of Social Sciences 1: 107
guard, consequences of letting down one's 2: 61
guidance 1: 9, 2: 108; advice to leaders offering 2: 67. *See also* fostering

Hankook Ilbo, "Koh Do-won's Morning Reflections" 1: 51
happiness 2: 26; building a life-state of 2: 108; endangering the path to 1: 90; finding true 2: 8, 25, 66, 68; foundation for all 2: 33; fostering human 1: 44; foundation for 2: 4; Josei Toda stating time of attaining genuine 2: 32; key to 1: 56, 2: 45, 108; Nichiren Daishonin expounding path of finding true 1: 21; realizing absolute 2: 51; spreading 1: 41–42; way to 1: 62
Hardenberg, Friedrich Leopold von. *See* Novalis
Harding, Vincent, and Soka Gakkai's movement 2: 106
hardships, attitude toward 2: 107; generating strength to overcome 1: 14

Harvard University 1: 129, 2: 20, 2: 52
Headquarters Leaders Meeting (35th), and Nichiren Shoshu priesthood 1: 123
health, attention to 2: 26, 107, 115; foundation to good 2: 57
Hei no Saemon, Nichiren Daishonin chiding 2: 14
Henderson, Hazel 1: 86
Himachal-Pradesh 1: 44
honesty 1: 46
honor, greatest of 1: 101; true 2: 44
hope 1: 78, 109; cause for limitless 1: 93, 2: 40; inspiring 2: 84; key to 2: 45; never lose 1: 107; source of 1: 80
Hugo, Victor 1: 10, 28, 2: 45, 68
human beings, benefit of attaining inner change in 2: 58; core quality of 1: 74
human revolution, Josei Toda declaring essence of 1: 29; way of life of 2: 77
humanism 1: 107
humanity, cause to manifest one's 2: 67; developing 1: 37; path of 2: 67; securing the future of 1: 90; welfare of 2: 47
Hunan Normal University 1: 107, 2: 55
Hunter, Howard, and 1991 excommunication of the Soka Gakkai 1:132
Huyghe, René, *Dawn After Dark* 1:132; and Soka Gakkai 1:132

Ichigaya 1: 55
ideals, high 1: 86. *See also* goals
ideas 2: 48
ignorance, Josei Toda on 2: 25
Ikeda, Daisaku, "The Age of
Soft Power" 2: 21; spirit of 2:
116; awards 2: 2, 109; *Boys'*
Adventure (later *Boys' Japan*)
2: 93; bringing happiness to
members, efforts in 2: 40;
peace proposal of 1: 2–3;
and devilish functions 2:
102; and fighting spirit 2: 83;
foundation 2: 11; health 1: 55
2: 3; Josei Toda' commitment
to 2: 3; Josei Toda's lesson to 1:
52; Josei Toda's strict training
of 2: 93–94; "Mahayana
Buddhism and Twenty-
first-Century Civilization"
2: 21; mind-set 2: 102;
Nichiren Shoshu priesthood,
dismissal by 1: 124–25, 128;
perceiving people's true
nature 1: 101; prayer 1: 10,
49, 57, 91, 136, 138, 2: 3–4,
37–38, 63; receiving honorary
doctorates from Mongolia
2: 110; resigning as third
president of the Soka Gakkai
2: 40; spirit 2: 58, 73; "Toda
University," training at 2:
65; unforgettable memory 2:
97–98; vow 2: 16; youth, spirit
as 1: 55, 63, 105, 2: 85, 101–02;
winning formula of 1: 21. *See*
also Daisaku Ikeda research
groups

Ikeda Peace Park, establishment
of 2: 110
impolite 1: 67
inactiveness, Josei Toda's
strictness toward 2: 115
India, SGI members of 1: 27
individual, becoming capable
2: 24; fostering 2: 17; guard
against ill-intentioned 2: 117;
Josei Toda describing corrupt
2: 116; opposing corrupt
2: 116; reason for regions
successes in fostering 2: 108–
09; value of 1: 115; self-serving
1: 30
ingrates, Josei Toda's warning
against, within Soka Gakkai
2: 25
ingratitude, guarding against 2:
57
initiative, taking personal 2: 86
injustice 1: 30, 80; Josei Toda
outlining quality needed
for fighting 2: 75; Nichiren
Daishonin's anger toward 1:
36; speaking out against 2: 30
inspiration, sources of 2: 89
Institute of Oriental Studies
(Russia) 2: 105
Institut de France 1: 97
integrity 2: 102
International Society for the
Sociology of Religion 1:131
Italy 2: 67
Izumi, Akinori 2: 112

Jambudvipa 1: 27
Japan, elderly population in 2:

120; birth rate in 2: 40, 120; elderly population in 2: 40; first Mongol invasion of 2: 109; path of, during military rule 1: 36

Japan Airlines flight, crash of 2: 111

Japan-China friendship, Daisaku Ikeda's efforts in promoting 2: 53–55

Japan-China Peace and Friendship Treaty 2: 53–54; Deng Xiaoping's efforts toward 2: 54; "hegemony issue" in 2: 53

Jefferson, Thomas 1: 37; on government 1: 46

job, Josei Toda's guidance about 1: 55

joy 2: 103; appreciating 1: 36; realizing profound 2: 102; spreading 1: 41–42

Juhachi Shiryaku (Compendium of Eighteen Histories) 2: 111

juniors, raising 2: 39

justice 1: 90, 118, 135, 2: 58; benefit of speaking out for 2: 72; force for 2: 45; Josei Toda on 2: 44–45; path to unending triumph of 2: 3; power of 2: 56; true champs of 1: 36; words of 2: 68

Kamakura 2: 109

Kamono, Yukio, priesthood's attack on the Soka Gakkai, comment of 1: 130–31

Kanazawa Seiryou University [formerly Kanazawa University of Economics], 130

Kansai members 2: 75

Kansai Soka Schools 1: 88

Kant, Immanuel 2: 56

karma, transforming negative 1: 110

Kautilya 2: 7

Kayo-kai members, Josei Toda encouraging 2: 81–82

"keep a close watch on politics and government," Josei Toda stating reason to 2: 14

Keller, Helen 1: 86; and human revolution 1: 85

Key, Ellen 1: 45; on courage 1: 46

king, Nichiren Daishonin describing role of 2: 14

King, Jr., Martin Luther 2: 106; on religion 1: 46

kinship, building personal 1: 18

Kissinger, Henry 2: 48

Ko Do-won 1: 52

Kobayashi-cho 1: 55

kosen-rufu 1: 1, 12, 102 2: 2, 45; advancing 1: 8, 21, 59, 2: 22–23; aim of 1: 93, 2: 86; basis for the second stage of 2: 37; benefit of dedicating to cause of 2: 86; benefit of exerting to realize 1: 31; benefit of leading 1: 102; cause for the decline of 2: 101; commitment to 2: 95; criteria for advancing 1: 63; Daisaku Ikeda renewing determination for worldwide 2: 41; driving forces of 1: 52; effect of struggling for 1: 110;

expanding 1: 31; foundation of 1: 83; future of 1: 34–35; goal of 1: 10; Josei Toda guarantees accomplishing of 1: 21; guarding against individuals destroying movement of 2: 117; Josei Toda describing benefit of life dedicated to 2: 68; Josei Toda highlighting path to 1: 99; Josei Toda outlining work of 2: 13; Josei Toda stating foundation in accomplishing 1: 53; Josei Toda stating purpose of 1:134; Josei Toda's advice for advancing 1: 112; Josei Toda's criteria to hasten 2: 12, 16; Josei Toda's forceful encouragement to accomplish, despite the times 2: 12; Josei Toda's remarks about members dedicated to 2: 116; key to expanding 2: 86–87; life dedicated to 1: 61, 63, 86–87, 95–97, 2: 26; movement for 1: 3; Nichiren Daishonin outlining obstruction to 1: 123; obstacles in advancing 2: 102, 117; path of 1: 37, 2: 44, 49; praising people dedicated to 1: 101; protecting people dedicated to 1: 101; starting point of 1:115; struggle for 1: 90, 2: 112; two wheels of 1: 52; upholding successors of 1: 91; victory and 1: 90; way to advance, exponentially 2: 5; worldwide 2: 84

Kufuor, John Agyekum 1: 61
Kusunoki Masashige 1: 108
Kyoto 1: 89, 131

lackluster 1: 67
Langley, Winston 1: 2–5; and Daisaku Ikeda 1: 3–5
lateness, Josei Toda's strictness about 2: 75
Latter Day of the Law, Buddhist practice for 1: 22
Latin America, *kosen-rufu* movement in 2: 41
leaders, action of 1: 8–9; basis to follow 2: 111; caring quality of 1: 54–55; characteristics of 1: 41; criteria for evaluating 2: 11; and devilish influences 2: 96; failure as 1: 67; fighting spirit of 1: 70; first priority as 2: 71–72; genuine 1: 8, 45, 92; guidelines to new 2: 113; hearts of 1: 12; hopes for 2: 8, 69, 94; hopes for the senior 2: 72; formula of ever-triumphant 1: 1; guidelines for newly appointed 2: 84; inner resolve of 1: 68; Josei Toda outlining qualities of good 2: 11–12; Josei Toda outlining role of 2: 25; Josei Toda's guidance to 2: 25; Josei Toda's strictness to 2: 15, 75; Josei Toda's warning to 1: 67–68; key to manifesting highest potential for 2: 46; *kosen-rufu* life for 2: 69; and life-condition 1: 49; need for 2: 46; and new

members 1: 17; qualities for male 1: 56, 59–60 2: 4, 5, 2: 38, 86–87, 104; qualities for 1: 11–13, 17, 19, 53–55, 63, 66–67, 70, 78, 82, 92, 95, 102, 109, 111–12, 115–16, 2: 12, 18–20, 31, 45–46, 51, 61, 67–68, 71–72, 74–76, 83, 86, 101, 103, 111–13, 116–17; responsibility of 1: 35, 50–51, 54, 2: 94, 96; responsibility of newly appointed 1: 35; responsibility of senior 1: 38; role of 2: 87; self-centered 2: 46; spirit for 1: 28, 2: 101; starting point in cultivating strength for 1: 49; true worth of 1: 28; victories 2: 103

leadership, effect of appointing new 1: 12; Josei Toda's comments on 1: 111–12; K'ung-ming's theories of 1: 66–75; universal truth of 2: 75

leadership positions 1: 20; Josei Toda's guidance to leaders about 2: 25; in the Soka Gakkai 2: 45–46

Leaves of Grass (Whitman) 1: 137

Leonardo, da Vinci, on ingratitude 2: 67

liars, Josei Toda on 2: 12; weeding out 2: 72

life 1: 7, 60 2: 8, 45; Buddhist way of 2: 67; choices in 1: 102; closing chapter of 1: 97, 117–18; embellishing 1: 80; enriching 2: 5; foundation of 1: 115; fulfillment in 1: 37, 99; honor in 2: 102; key to a

courageous 2: 46; living out 1: 137; pride in 2: 102; success in 1: 99; treasure in 1: 13; victory in 1: 42

lighthearted, Tsunesaburo Makiguchi's formula to remain 1: 50

Likimani, Muthoni 1: 107

limitations, Josei Toda outlining determination to break through self-imposed 2: 17

listening 1: 53, 66, 115, 2: 101

Little Lord Fauntleroy (Burnett) 2: 82

Liu Ch'an, K'ung-ming's loyalty to 1: 69

Liu Pei 1: 65, 69

"living faith" 1: 44

losing 1: 102, 2: 103

Lotus Sutra, Nichiren Daishonin outlining enemies of 1: 119–20; Nichiren Daishonin outlining pattern of persecution for practitioners of 1: 118–19; Nichiren Daishonin outlining quality for practitioners of 2: 101; Nichiren Daishonin stating persecutions in propagating 1: 101; Nichiren Daishonin's passages of proof outlining effects of slandering practitioners of 2: 23–24; Nichiren Daishonin's warning about the enemies of 2: 61; Nichiren Daishonin's warning against despising practitioners of 2: 82; Nichiren Daishonin's warning to believers in 2: 95

Lu Xun 2: 8, 19; denouncing injustice 2: 55–56

Lycée Henri IV (secondary school) 2: 33

Makiguchi, Tsunesaburo 1: 33, 42, 2: 26; arrest 2: 47, 73; betrayal of 2: 73; Buddhist practice 1: 8; and devilish functions 2: 13; faith of the Soka Gakkai leaders at time of 2: 117; favorite Chinese maxim of 1: 19; great evil, observation of 1:133; and greatness 2: 17; the High Priest, audience with 2: 47; on Josei Toda 2: 47; Josei Toda and 1: 14; Josei Toda outlining funeral service of 2: 73; Josei Toda's determination to vindicate 2: 73–74; Josei Toda expressing gratitude to 2: 73; Josei Toda's remarks at sixth memorial (fifth anniversary) of 2: 73; Josei Toda's wrath against leaders betraying 1: 98; Nichiren Buddhism, dedication to 1: 38; priesthood, anger against 2: 47; receiving benefits from practicing Nichiren Buddhism 1: 38; Shinto talisman, refusing 2: 47; spirit 2: 58; street and parks named after 1: 82–83; *The System of Value-Creating Education* [*Soka kyoikugaku taikei*] 1: 45; and *Theory of Value* 2: 73; "We youth" phrase used by 1: 96

Malaysia, SGI members in 2: 41

"many in body, one in mind" 1: 35, 61; spirit of 1: 44, 102, 116 2: 6, 71

Marinoff, Lou 1: 106

marriage, Josei Toda advising young women's division members on 2: 65–66

Matsuno Rokuro Saemon 1: 118

Maurois, André 1: 53

Mazzini, Giuseppe (champion of Italian independence) 2: 68

McLennan Jr., William, the Soka Gakkai, remarks about 2: 52

"meeting revolution" 1: 9

meetings, ending 1: 91–92

member care, significance of 2: 116

members, action of leaders toward suffering 1: 41, behavior of leaders toward 1: 41–42; bonds with 1: 49; characteristic needed to protect fellow 2: 101; effect of betraying fellow 2: 7; factors necessary to initiate momentum among 2: 75–76; hopes for 2: 8; key to protecting 1: 56; protecting 1: 21; reason for fostering new 2: 108; supporting 1: 115–16

men's division, earning trust of, by the youth division 1: 43; role of 1: 59; spirit of 2: 76–77

men's division leaders, appreciating 2: 22

mentor, effect of betraying 2: 7

mentor-disciple relationship,
Daisaku Ikeda's reason to
advance the path of 2: 3–4;
Josei Toda outlining 2: 17, 72;
Nichiren Daishonin outlining
2: 2; significance of studying
spirit of 2; 108; spirit 1: 14, 33–
34 2: 7, 73–74; true Soka spirit
of 2: 11; to youth division 2: 16
mentors 2: 2
Milton, John 1: 31; on ingratitude
2: 67
mind, frame of 1: 11; inspiring
peace of 2: 83; Nichiren
Daishonin expounding power
of 1: 35
mind-set 1: 46; overcoming fixed
1: 96
misery, basis of human 1: 44
misfortune, path to 1: 60
mission 1: 37, 95–96; benefits of
realizing one's 1: 74; carrying
out one's 2: 46; place of 1: 14;
unique 2: 108
Mitchell, Donald 1: 105
momentum 2: 106
Mongolia, Nichiren Daishonin
lamenting execution of the
envoys of 2: 109–10; Soka
Gakkai representatives visit
to 2: 109
Mongolia-Japan relations, Soka
Gakkai's contribution toward
2: 109–10
Mongolian University of Arts
and Culture 2: 109
Morita, Kazuya, Nikken's
behavior toward 1: 124

mothers 1: 28
motivation, inspiring 2: 84
Mount Minobu 1: 23
Mukherjee, Bharati 2: 2
Mystic Law 1: 60, 2: 51; benefit
of practicing 1: 118; life
dedicated to 2: 2; Nichiren
Daishonin expounding
benefit of propagating 1: 100;
Nichiren Daishonin stating
benefit of propagating 2:
86; Nichiren Daishonin's
instructions to rely on 1: 43;
power of 1: 11, 2: 45, 108;
securing path for prosperity of
2: 22–23; scope of 1: 95

Nagarjuna, on gratitude 2: 105
Nagashima, Danny 2: 51;
achievements under
leadership of 2: 79–81
Nanjo Tokimitsu 1: 92
Nam-myoho-renge-kyo 2: 48;
chanting of 2: 49; Josei Toda
stating benefit of chanting 1:
23. *See also* Mystic Law
National Language Bureau, of
SGI-USA 2: 80
nationalism 1: 5
nations, causes for failure of 1:
81–82; criteria for growth and
prosperity of 1: 45; foundation
for building trust among
1: 93; prosperity of 1: 67;
treasure of 2: 43; Tsunesaburo
Makiguchi highlighting factor
threatening the future of 1: 36
Nationwide Executive

Conference, Daisaku Ikeda's expressing gratitude at 2: 1, 71

Nazis 2: 23, 48

negative forces, benefit to battle 2: 102; effect of not confronting, mirrors "betraying the Buddha's teaching" 2: 13

negligence 1: 9; leaders and 2: 56

New Orleans, opening of the SGI Community Center in 2: 51; honors Daisaku Ikeda 2: 52; honors SGI members 2: 52; Ikedas visit to 2: 52

Nichijun, and Soka Gakkai 1: 122

Nichikan 1: 27

Nichiren Buddhism 1: 8; basic principle in 2: 117; benefit of practicing 1: 87, 112; benefit of propagating 2: 115; correct practice for practitioners of 1: 22; essence of 1: 50, 116, 2: 46; heart of 2: 3; Josei Toda's confidence about 1: 31; Nichiren Daishonin's admonition to practitioners of 1: 22; spirit of practitioners of 2: 101; teachings of 1: 24, 109, 2: 72, 97; Tsunesaburo Makiguchi reminding intent of 1: 24; universality of 2: 69; westward transmission of 1: 27; world leaders and 1: 31

Nichiren Daishonin, aim of 2: 29; aspiration of 1: 37; basis of writing style of 2: 89–90; "Conversation between a Sage and an Unenlightened Man"

2: 64; criteria in finding spirit of 1: 23; "Encouragement to a Sick Person" 2: 95; "On Establishing the Correct Teaching for the Peace of the Land" 1: 36; "On the Four Stages of Faith and the Five Stages of Practice" 2: 82; goal entrusted to practitioners by 2: 6; happiness 2: 110; legacy 1: 7; "The Letter of Petition from Yorimoto" 1: 119; "Letter from Sado" 1: 134, 2: 95; "Letter from Teradomari" 2: 96; "Letter to the Brothers" 2: 95; "Letter to Konichi-bo" 2: 61; lion's roar of, 101; "Many in Body, One in Mind" 2: 23; "Omens" 1: 119; and pattern of obstacle 2: 7; "On Practicing the Buddha's Teaching" 1: 22; and propagation 1: 37; "Questions and Answers about Embracing the Lotus Sutra" 2: 23, 63; "On Reciting the Daimoku of the Lotus Sutra" 2: 97; *The Record of the Orally Transmitted Teachings* 1: 109; "Response to the Petition from Gyobin" 1: 119; "The Selection of the Time" 1: 119, 2: 23; "The Votary of the Lotus Sutra Will Meet Persecution" 2: 96; "What It Means to Slander the Law" 2: 97; wish of 1: 27; "The Workings of Brahma and Shakra" 2: 90

Nichiren Shoshu priesthood,

behavior of, matches
Shakyamuni's describing
one type of ascetic 2: 110–11;
cause for the spiritual decay
of 2: 38; greedy nature of
1: 121; and Josei Toda, 127;
path of 1: 88; peculiarity of
1: 133 "Questions Regarding
the Speech of Honorary
President Ikeda at the 35th
Headquarters Leaders
Meeting" 1: 123; scheme of 1:
122–26; and *shakubuku* 2: 30;
Soka Gakkai's contribution to
1: 122; Soka Gakkai's petition
and 1:128; and Tsunesaburo
Makiguchi 1: 127
Nichiren, writings of 2: 61, 67;
Josei Toda's emphasis on
reading 2: 17; reading 2: 17–18
Nightingale, Florence 1: 46
Nikken 1: 88, 122, 125–26; and
behavior 1: 122; being "double
tongued," example of, 122–24;
"contradicting his own
words" example of 1: 122–24;
Daisaku Ikeda's leadership,
praising 1: 124; praising Soka
Gakkai 1: 124; retribution
1:133
Nikko Shonin 1: 23
Nissho, and Soka Gakkai 1:122
Nittatsu, and Soka Gakkai 1: 122
Nomonhan, Battle of 2: 110
Norton, David, priesthood's
attack on the Soka Gakkai,
views of 1: 129; the
priesthood's Notice of

Excommunication, comments
about 1: 129
Novalis 1: 116
Nkrumah, Kwame 1: 61

obstacles, benefit of overcoming
1: 110; encountering 1: 101
"obstacles equal peace and
comfort," in practice 1: 60
Oceania, *kosen-rufu* movement
in 2: 41
oneness of mentor and disciple
1: 28
Operation C, aim of 1: 122.
See also Nichiren Shoshu
priesthood
Operation Tanuki Festival 1: 127
opinions, leaders and 2: 51
opponents, Nichiren Daishonin's
unyielding conviction against
1: 100; Nichiren Daishonin's
view of 1: 99–100
opportunities, seizing 1: 66
optimistic 2: 107
organizations 1: 21; basis for
growth of 2: 19–20,104; cause
for stagnation of 2: 20; cause
for the decline of 2: 56; causes
for failure of 1: 81–82; criteria
for growth and prosperity of
1: 45; decline of, 2: 38; factors
to advance growth of 2: 31;
growth of 1: 67; Josei Toda
stating reason for protecting
1: 20; mark of humanistic
1: 46; and reform 2: 20;
requirements for successful
1: 71; spirit for growth of 2:

107; warning signs for decline
of 1: 70
Osaka campaign and Daisaku
Ikeda 2: 75
Osaka Incident 1: 33; 2: 3
Oxford University 1:131, 2: 20, 48

parents, behavior toward 1:
92–93; Nichiren Daishonin's
guidance on treating 1: 92
Paris, fall of 2: 48
Passbook Number F. 47927
(Likimani) 1: 107
passion, highest form of 2: 49
peace 2: 6, 47; endangering the
path to 1: 90; path to 2: 84
peace of mind, source of 2: 89
people 1: 91; building force of
capable, for *kosen-rufu* 1: 49;
consequences of not raising
new 1: 53; egoistic 2: 67; era
of 1: 8; gathering support of
1: 8; K'ung-ming's criteria
for selecting gifted 1: 71–72;
K'ung-ming's warning to
distance oneself from five
kinds of 1: 73; raising capable
1: 18, 35; and Soka Gakkai 2:
44; vitalizing 2: 76; winning
the hearts of 1: 53–54
Perestroika Library and Archives
1: 90
persecutions 1: 79; cause of
1: 119; Josei Toda's faith
during 2: 117; Nichiren
Daishonin views 1: 101;
Soka Gakkai leaders faith
during 2: 117; Tsunesaburo

Makiguchi outlining benefit of
experiencing 1:134; un-scared
of 2: 47
perseverance, 82
Plato 1: 37, 112, 117; on sleep 2: 57
*Plato, Not Prozac!:Applying Eternal
Wisdom to Everyday Problems*
(Marinoff) 1: 106
politicians, hypocrisy of 2: 104;
Josei Toda describing corrupt
2: 14; Josei Toda outlining role
of 2: 14; self-centered 2: 104;
spirit of 2: 105
politics, corrupt nature of 2: 7;
Josei Toda encouraging Soka
Gakkai members entering 2:
15; Patricio Aylwin's remarks
about elevating quality of 2:
105
positions, handling changes in
organizational 2: 39
potential, Josei Toda outlines the
way to tap into our true 2: 17
power, greatest 1: 109; people
and 1: 5–6
practice 1: 37, 2: 117; courageous
2: 43; earnest 2: 51; Nichiren
Daishonin emphasizing 2:
39; power of 1: 117; steadfast
2: 89
practitioner, courageous 1: 121
praise 1: 116; Tsunesaburo
Makiguchi on 1: 62
prayer 1: 91, 115; benefit of
earnest 2: 108; earnest 1: 28,
2: 38, 2: 120; effect of 1: 108;
powerful weapon of 1: 102;
resolute 1: 88, 2: 38

presidents, heart of Soka Gakkai
2: 58–59
pride 2: 48
priests, corrupt 1: 119; Nichiren
Daishonin guaranteeing
Buddhahood for taking
on evil 1: 134; Nichiren
Daishonin outlining nature
f false 1: 125
problems 1: 31
progress, key to 2: 45
propagation, and Daisaku Ikeda
2: 31; emphasis on, 31; and
Josei Toda 1: 52; Lotus Sutra
outlines the obstacles in
conducting 2: 30; Nichiren
Daishonin outlining goal of
2: 5–6; and persecution 2: 30;
Tsunesaburo Makiguchi on 1:
23. See also shakubuku
Protestant Reformation, 129
publications, benefit of increasing
circulation of 2: 31; and Josei
Toda 1: 52
Pumpkin 2: 109
Purdue University 1: 106
purpose, feeling a sense of 1: 36

Rabindra Bharati University of
Kolkata (Calcutta) 2: 2
Ramakrishna 2: 2
'refute the erroneous and reveal
the true," spirit 2: 30
On the Republic (Cicero) 1: 77
"refuting the erroneous and
revealing the true" spirit of
1: 30
region leader, role of 1: 2

relationship, benefit of fantastic
2: 5
religion, features of world
2: 97–98; finding highest
philosophy of 2:16; hallmark
of genuine 2: 69; Josei Toda
outlining function of genuine
1: 112; true 1: 46; Tsunesaburo
Makiguchi describing mission
of 1: 24, 50
Religious Nongovernmental
Organizations, representatives
of 2: 81; SGI representative in
2: 81
Renaissance, birthplace of 2: 67
report, timely 2: 18–19
Republic, The (Plato) 1: 37
retirement, in Buddhism 1: 37, 96;
in life 1: 37, 96
resolve, half-hearted 1: 101; inner
1: 35–36
respect, gaining 2: 117; people of
highest 2: 64
responsibilities 1: 62; break down
1: 59
retiree, encouragement to 1: 96
revolutionary, mark of a true 2:
2, 24
Rizal, José 2: 58
Rolland, Romain 2: 2
Romance of the Three Kingdoms,
The 1: 14, 54, 65
Rome, Daisaku Ikeda composing
a poem in 1: 81
Roosevelt, Eleanor 1: 87
Roosevelt, Franklin Delano
1: 87
rumors, handling 1: 9

Russia 1; 89; and SGI members
2: 26
Ryokan, modern-day 1: 126
(*See also* Nikken); Nichiren
Daishonin describing
cowardly manner of 1: 124–25;
Nichiren Daishonin outlining
true nature of 1: 125; Nichiren
Daishonin records fate of
1:133

Sado Island 1: 97
Saito, Kenji 2: 112
Sakurai, Hiro appointed as
committee president of
Religious Nongovernmental
Organizations 2: 81
Sammi-bo, Buddhist practice
2: 120; Nichiren Daishonin
records the fate of 2: 120
Schiller, Friedrich von 2: 6, 93
Schopenhauer, Arthur, on envy
1: 31
seeking spirit 2: 89
Seikyo Shimbun 1: 2, 53; aim of
2: 31; Josei Toda affirming
mission of 1: 52
self-improvement, key to
2: 3; limitless 1: 31, 2: 72;
Tsunesaburo Makiguchi on
1: 31
senior members, source of pride
for 2: 39
sense of responsibility,
manifesting 1: 91
SGI, goal of 1: 20–21; growth of
1: 105; implications of growth
of 1: 37; and Josei Toda 1: 21;

mission of 1: 9; reason for
development of 2: 107–08;
significance of betraying 1:132;
spirit of, 28; 30th anniversary
of 1: 97; world leaders and
1: 31
SGI activities, benefit of carrying
out 2: 4
SGI-Italy 1: 82
SGI members, mission of 2: 45;
strength of 2: 48
SGI movement 1: 2
SGI organizations, causes
for decline of 1: 19; and
Nichiren Shoshu priesthood's
intimidations 1: 125–26
SGI Plaza 2: 80
SGI-South Korea (KSGI),
development of 2: 41
SGI-USA, Culture of Peace
for the Children of the
World exhibition of 2: 80;
development of 2: 41; growth
and development of 2: 79–81;
resource centers of 2: 80–81
SGI-USA New York Culture
Center 2: 80
Shakespeare, William 2: 57
shakubuku 1: 31; emphasis on
practicing 1: 23; Josei Toda
expounding benefits of
practicing 1: 23; leaders and
2: 29; Nichiren Daishonin and
2: 29; Nichiren Daishonin
expounding effects of
practicing 1: 22; purpose of 2:
29; spirit of 1: 83
Shakyamuni Buddha, final

words of 2: 38; and pattern of obstacle 2: 7; and propagation 1: 37

Shariputra, Nichiren Daishonin clarifying enlightenment of 2: 64

Shijo Kingo 1: 120; Nichiren Daishonin's concern and 1:128

silence 1: 11, 41

sincerity 1: 78, 2: 102; genuine 2: 31

Singapore, SGI members in 2: 41

slander, uprooting 2: 72

slanderers, benefit of rebuking 2: 90; Nichiren Daishonin outlining effects of not admonishing 1: 135; Shakyamuni describing 2: 119

society 1: 1, 20, 50, 78, 2: 30; cause for decline of 2: 105; power to transforming 1: 35; preserving goodness of 1: 30; securing integrity of 1: 30

Soka, life of 1: 38; scope of 1: 116; way of 2: 63; world of 1: 117

Soka Bodhi Tree Garden 1: 27. See also India

Soka Gakkai, action against leaders abusing 2: 87; action against obstructing advance of 2: 96; activities of, in accord with the Daishonin's teachings 2; 96–97; aim of 2: 87; attaining victory in 2: 51; basis for advancing 1: 18, 2: 74; basis for victories of 1: 88 2: 6–7, 86; and Buddhism 1: 8; cause for possible decline of 2:

64; cause for demise of 2: 72; cause for development of 1: 1, 34–35; cause for development and growth of 2: 116; cause for growth of 2: 19–20; causes for advancement of 2: 120; cause for stagnation of 2: 103; center of 2: 38–39; characteristics of, 2: 90; characteristics of people betraying 1: 61; core of 2: 72; Daisaku Ikeda's action against criticizing 2: 101; Daisaku Ikeda's efforts in protecting 2: 62–63; Daisaku Ikeda's vision for 1: 49; effect of leaving 2: 95; effect of making negative causes against 2: 7; effect of slandering 2: 25; eightieth anniversary of 2: 37, 41,61; essence of 1: 19, 34, 2: 24; eternal spirit of 1: 14; exemplary priests and 1: 129; factor that will confirm the future 2: 103; focus of 2: 17; foundation of 2: 29, 39, 61, 64; future of 2: 82; growth and development of 1:133; and head temple 1: 23–24; heart of 1: 34, 2: 38; history of 1: 102, 2: 85; inheritance of 1: 120; in Japan 1: 105; Josei Toda declaring consequences of betraying 1:134; Josei Toda describing cause of decline of 2: 25; Josei Toda describing goal of 1: 20; Josei Toda describing strength of 1: 21–22, 2:13; Josei Toda describing three kinds of people in 2: 76; Josei Toda outlining aim of 2: 15–16; Josei Toda outlining group causing problems for 2: 76; Josei Toda outlining spirit of 1:134; Josei Toda expounding mission of 1: 23; Josei Toda proclaiming 2: 30; Josei Toda revealing factors for achieving result in 2: 25; key to success of 1: 109; leadership guide for leaders of 1: 54; lifeblood of 2: 24; mission of 1: 5–6, 117, 126 2: 2; Notice of Excommunication and 1: 121, 128; path of 2: 47, 51; and people 1: 95; people in 2: 24, 117; persecutions of 2: 30; persecutions faced by, indicated in Nichiren's writings 1: 120–21; persecutions of, predicted in Lotus Sutra 1: 120–21; philosophy of 1: 54; purpose of 1: 83–84, 2: 46, 108; reason for global development of 2: 4; school of 1: 95; securing foundation of 1: 17; seventy-fifth anniversary of 1: 97, 2: 37, 38, 41, 44, 71, 115; seventy-third anniversary of 1:133; significance of progress of 2: 110; significance of studying the history of 2: 108; sixtieth anniversary of 1: 120, 123; soul of 1: 14; source of growth and development of 1: 42; spirit of 1: 18–19, 36, 2: 39, 45,

55; spirit to advance goals of 2: 51, 98, 106, 115; stage of 1: 34, 2: 41; strength of 2: 108, 116; success of 1: 71; theme of, in 2002 1: 38; tradition in 1: 78, 2: 5, 11–12, 19, 39, 76, 108; Tsunesaburo Makiguchi highlighting organizational matters of 1: 62; way to protect 2: 83; world of 2: 64; world thinkers' hopes for 2: 98; youth and 1: 22

Soka Gakkai activities 1: 49; benefit of carrying out 2: 26; benefit of involving in 1: 95–96; changing format of 2: 30; changing structure of 2: 30

Soka Gakkai Headquarters Leaders Meeting 1: 121, 123

Soka Gakkai members, awards and honors on 2: 44; characteristics of 2: 117; and communities 2: 112; hopes for 2: 44, 68–69; Josei Toda declaring consequences of slandering 2: 23; mission of 2: 63. *See also* members

Soka Gakkai's education department members, gratitude to 2: 22

Soka humanism, interest in 1: 106; network of 2: 26

Soka members, description of 1: 115

Soka University of America, achievements of the first class of graduates of 2: 79; aim of 2: 120; fifth entering class of

2: 120; hopes for 1: 33–34;
opening of 2: 120; plans for
tenth anniversary of 2: 120
Soka women, Daisaku Ikeda's
expressing gratitude to 2: 86
solidarity 1: 61
Soong, Ching-ling 1: 9, 90, 102;
the youth, message to, 91;
women of Asia, message to 1:
91; youth, message to 1: 91
Sophocles 1:137, 2: 7
Sorbonne University 2: 20
South China Normal University
1: 107
speech 1: 78
speaking up, consequences for
leaders not 1: 50–51
spirit, fighting 1: 70, 97, 2: 103;
high 1: 71; maintaining a
youthful 1: 96; Nichiren
Daishonin outlining
fundamental 2: 29; strong 1: 60
spiritual evolution, Winston
Langley's views of achieving
1: 4
spirituality, leaders and 2: 49;
nations and 2: 49; Winston
Langley and 1: 5
Staël, Madame de 1: 87–88, 107,
2: 49, 57
stagnation 2: 2; cause of 1: 74
stalemate, breakthrough 2: 40
stand alone spirit 1: 96; power of
1: 45
Stanford University 2: 52
status, social 2: 64, 68
strength, deriving 2: 46; Nichiren
Daishonin emphasizing 1: 56;

source of 1: 80, 137; testing
2: 56
striving, benefit of 2: 26
strong 2: 46; becoming 2: 8
student division leaders,
appreciating 2: 22
study 2: 38–39, 117; leaders and
1: 19; Nichiren Daishonin
emphasizing 2: 39; purpose of
2: 62; and youth division 2: 39
Su Shih 1: 11–12
SUA (Soka University of
America) graduates, hope for
2: 79. *See also* Soka University
of America
sufferings, Josei Toda
highlighting factors in
overcoming 1: 23
Summer training sessions,
rhythm of 2: 19
Sun Ch'üan 1: 65
Sun, Yat-sen 1: 9, 90, 102
support, mutual 2: 120
symbiosis, Winston Langley and,
1: 3–4

Tagore, Rabindranath 2: 2
Taiheiki (Chronicle of the Great
Peace) 1: 108
Taiseki-ji (Nichiren Shoshu head
temple), and land reforms
1: 122; and priesthood
abolishing Soka Gakkai-
operated pilgrimages to 1:
126; 700th anniversary of
founding of 1: 122; Shizuoka
youth division's role in
700th anniversary of 1: 122;

significance of priesthood's terminating Soka Gakkai-operated pilgrimages to 1: 128; Soka Gakkai-operated pilgrimages to 1: 122, 127

Take, Kuniyasu, priesthood's attack on Soka Gakkai, comment on 1:131

"Teacher of the Law" chapter (Lotus Sutra) 1: 120

Teacher's College 1: 33

teachers, role of 2: 121

teaching, Nichiren Daishonin outlining factor to evaluate correct 2: 46

tenacity 1: 82

thinkers, Daisaku Ikeda's reason for quoting words of world 1: 43–44

Thomson, James 2: 58

thoughts, cause of negative 2: 61

three bodies of the Buddha, concept of 1: 109

three obstacles and four devils 2: 102, 117

three powerful enemies, cause for appearance of 1: 110; Nichiren Daishonin outlining characteristics of third of 1: 125

three thousand realms in a single moment of life, concept of 1: 11, 35

three types of enemies, Nichiren Daishonin warns disciples against 1: 100

T'ien't'ai 2: 29

times, transforming 2: 68

Tochigi Prefecture 2: 65

Toda, Josei 1: 1, 18, 54, 63, 85, 115, 2: 26, 111; admonishment 2: 48; Buddhist practice 1: 8; business 2: 64; commitment 2: 11; on Daisaku Ikeda 1: 42, 2: 2, 65; Daisaku Ikeda on 1: 33; Daisaku Ikeda's action against people slandering 2: 101; Daisaku Ikeda's devotion to 2: 74; and Daisaku Ikeda's personal struggles 2: 74; and devilish functions 2: 13; "Epigrams" 1: 127; greatest joy 1: 111; and greatness 2: 17; and guidance 2: 12; and human being 1: 112, 118; *Human Revolution, The* 2: 17; inaugurated as second president of Soka Gakkai 2: 74; inheritance 1: 101; prison, mind-set in 2: 46; realization 1: 29; ruling, 41; on Soka Gakkai organization 2: 24; spirit 1: 118, 2: 18; mind-set in 2: 46; spirit 2: 58; vow 2: 74; wish 2: 11, 24; and white lilies 2: 43; youth division about *kosen-rufu*, instructions to 1: 42

Tokyo Soka Junior High School, accomplishment of 1: 77

Tokyo Soka Senior High School, accomplishment of 1: 77

Toller, Ernst 1: 11

Tolstoy, Leo 1: 60–61, 96; on suffering 1: 31

Toynbee, Arnold J. 2: 97; basis for dialogue between Daisaku

Ikeda and 2: 98; Daisaku Ikeda's impression of 2: 98
training, benefit of strict, 2: 94; youth division members and 2: 94
traitors 1: 51; Josei Toda's warning against, within Soka Gakkai 2: 25; Tsunesaburo Makiguchi describing fate of 1:134
"true mission" 1: 29
trust 2: 67; building 1: 18; creating mutual , between senior and junior members 2: 5; Daisaku Ikeda's remarks about 1: 52; foundation for building 1: 93; Josei Toda on 1: 53; Josei Toda's advice for gaining, in society 1: 112; way for leaders to win people's 2: 102
truth 1: 44; benefit of speaking out for 2: 72; conveying 1: 90; defeating 2: 45; gaining 2: 117; labeling people against defending 1: 80; path to unending triumph of 2: 3; power of 2: 56; speaking out for 1: 112, 2: 47; weapon of 1:137; words of 2: 68
Ts'ao Ts'ao 1: 65
Tsedev, Dojoogiin 2: 109
Tufts University 1:132
twentieth century, human life in 1: 3
twenty-first century, 3; hopes for, 97; human society in 1: 3
2010, Soka Gakkai in 2: 37

understanding, way for leaders to gain people's 2: 102
unfocused, effect of being 1: 61; Josei Toda's strictness toward 2: 115
universities, and capable people 2: 120; study of SGI's philosophy in, 105–06
University of Bologna 1: 82, 2: 67
University of Denver 2: 106
University of Massachusetts 1: 2
unity 1: 1, 71, 2: 18, 48; basis for true 1: 44; building 1: 55; creating mutual, between senior and junior members 2: 5; guarding against individuals destroying 2: 117; Josei Toda and 1: 116; need for 2: 6; Nichiren Daishonin describing importance of maintaining 2: 96; Nichiren Daishonin outlining benefit of 1: 61
Unkart-Seifert, Jutta 1: 108
Ushio (magazine) 2: 21, 104

value, key to achieving new 1: 59
value creation, life of 2: 33
victors, 1: 46, 85–86; Nichiren Daishonin describing 1: 7
victory 1: 28, 102, 2: 106; Buddhist formula for 1: 61; cause for 1: 7; cause for daily 2: 115; creating cause for next 2: 56; determining, under adverse conditions 1: 108–09; driving force for 1: 137; formula for 2: 51; Josei Toda stating cause for

1: 1; key to 1: 82, 2: 48, 89; key
to all 2; 38; key to eternal 2: 56;
Nichiren Daishonin outlining
strategy for 2: 112; path to 1:
61, 102, 2: 18, 51, 112; Soka
Gakkai 2: 45
vitality 2: 103; source of limitless
2: 2
Vivekananda, Swami 2: 2
voice, Nichiren Daishonin
describing function of, 41;
Nichiren outlining importance
of 2: 83; Nichiren Daishonin
outlining power of using 1:
116; power of using 1: 51;
types of 1: 115
Vorobyova-Desyatovskaya,
Margarita, and people's
government 2: 105–06
votary of the Lotus Sutra,
hallmarks of 1: 120–21;
Nichiren Daishonin describing
obstacles of 2: 30
vow 1: 28

Wang Anshi 2: 6
war, avoiding 1: 5–6; root of 1: 5
warmhearted 1: 93. *See also*
compassion
wealth, material 2: 68
Weil, Simone 2: 69; altruistic
outlook of 2: 34; birth 2: 33;
challenging deep-rooted
prejudices against women 2:
35–36; concerns 2: 35; death 2:
35; declaration 2: 36; education
2: 33; *Gravity and Grace* 2: 35;
health 2: 33–34; Joan of Arc

and 2: 34; *The Needs for Roots* 2:
35; *Oppression and Liberty* 2: 35;
qualities of 2: 34; and Spanish
Civil War 2: 35; during World
War II 2: 35
Whitman, Walt 1:137, 2: 89
Wilson, Bryan, Human Values
in a Changing World: A
Dialogue on the Social
Role of Religion 1:131; and
lay leadership in religion
1:132; 1991 priesthood's
excommunication of Soka
Gakkai, views of 1:131; Soka
Gakkai-operated pilgrimages,
views of 1:131–32
winning 1: 102, 2: 103; Josei Toda
on 2: 44; over yourself, 109;
reason for 1: 51
wisdom 2: 64; cause for limitless
1: 93; effect of 1: 108;
emergence of 1: 62
women, action against leaders for
discriminating 2: 87; benefit of
valuing 2: 104; role of 1: 107;
Shakyamuni Buddha and 2:
88; and twenty-first century 1:
45; valuing 1: 45, 2: 86
women disciples, expressing
gratitude to Shakyamuni
Buddha 2: 89; guidelines
regarding travel for, in
Shakyamuni's Order 2: 88–89
women's division, attitude of
male leaders to 2: 86–87;
altruistic spirit of 2: 35;
appreciating 2: 87; benefits of
efforts of 1: 87; Daisaku Ikeda

praising 1: 57, 88; earning the trust of, by youth division 1: 43; efforts of 2: 4, 43, 86–87; hopes for 1: 46; Josei Toda cheering activities of 1: 56–57; Josei Toda encouraging 1: 56; and leaders response time 2: 5; male leaders and 2: 38; men's attitude to 2: 4–5; praising 2: 87; respecting 1: 13, 28 2: 86; "radiance" of 1: 87; role of 1: 59; spirit of 2: 76–77; and white lilies 2: 43; youth division and 1: 12

women's division leaders, appreciating 2: 22; priority of 2: 89

words 1: 115

words and letters, Nichiren Daishonin stating importance of using, for *kosen-rufu* 2: 31

work, consequences for leaders avoiding hard 2: 102–03

works, Daisaku Ikeda reasoning for sharing words of great 2: 89

world, reason being born in 1: 108

world peace 1: 83; eternal path to 1: 102. *See also kosen-rufu*

World Tribune, growth of 2: 80

World War II, 2: 48; Japanese economy and society after 2: 12

Yalman, Nur, and Soka Gakkai reform movement 1: 129

Yamatai [ancient Japanese kingdom] 1: 5

Year of Glory and Great Victory (2003), Daisaku Ikeda expressing gratitude to members in 1: 117

years, determining factor in the final 2: 32

Yokota, Masao 2: 52

young men's division leaders, and challenges 2: 85; spirit of 2: 86

youth, call to 2: 116; challenge apt for 2: 84; developing 1: 12; hopes for 2: 8, 76; Josei Toda's call to 2: 44; path of 2: 44; period of 1: 91; power of 2: 16; power of energy of 2: 116; quality for 2: 72; raising 2: 72; role of 1: 12; spirit of, 21; training of 2: 33, 121; treasure of 1: 52

youth division, challenge for 1: 30; Daisaku Ikeda's commitment to 1: 53; efforts of 2: 4; encouragement to 1: 117–18; greatest life for 2: 36; growth of 2: 32; hallmark of 2: 102; hopes for 1: 34, 2: 16, 37–38, 83, 91, 113; and injustice 1: 36; Josei Toda and 2: 32; Josei Toda declaring spirit of 1: 29, 33–34; Josei Toda stating basis for attaining true greatness to 2: 12; Josei Toda encouraging 2: 16; Josei Toda's hopes for 1: 22; and *kosen-rufu* 1: 33; mission of 2: 37; and propagation 2: 32; silence and, 11; and Soka Gakkai meetings

1: 34; spirit of 2: 85; stage for, in the twenty-first century 1: 42–43; traditions of the Soka Gakkai's 2: 85; training of 1: 34; treasure for, 43
youth division leaders, behavior of, 18–19; qualities of, 82
youthful spirit, proof of maintaining 1: 96
young women's division, altruistic spirit of 2: 35; appreciating 2: 87; attitude of male leaders to 2: 86–87; Daisaku Ikeda's praising 1: 57, 88; effect of growth and development of 2: 103; efforts of 2: 86–87; growth of 2: 43; development of 2: 66; guidelines to 1: 92; hopes for 1: 46, 2: 16, 103–04; importance of fostering 2: 81–82; Josei Toda and, 34; Josei Toda applauding activities of 1: 56–57; Josei Toda encouraging 2: 13, 15–16, 65–66; Josei Toda highlighting mission of 2: 82–83; Josei Toda outlining way of life for 2: 82; Josei Toda's hopes for 1: 66, 2: 82–83; and leaders' response time 2: 5; male leaders and 2: 38; men's attitude to 2: 5; mission of 2: 103; potential of 2: 81–82; power of 2: 103; praising 2: 87; respecting 2: 86, 103; role of 1: 34–35; valuing 2: 103; women's division role toward 2: 87
young women's division leaders, priority of 2: 89
Yubari Coal Miners Union Incident 1: 33

Zhaoqing University 2: 55
Zhou Enlai 1: 69; 2: 1, 53; death 2: 54
Zhuge Liang. *See* Chuko K'ung-ming

More Reading on Nichiren Buddhism

FROM MIDDLEWAY PRESS

These titles can be purchased from your local or online
bookseller, or go to the Middleway Press Web site
(www.middlewaypress.com):

The Living Buddha: An Interpretive Biography
By DAISAKU IKEDA
The first in the three-volume Soka Gakkai History
of Buddhism series
An intimate portrayal of one of history's most important and
obscure figures, the Buddha, The Living Buddha chronicle reveals
him not as a mystic but as a warm and engaged human being who
was very much the product of his turbulent times. This is a biography with a double focus. It is a vivid historial narrative based on
what is known or can reasonably be surmised concerning the Buddha's life and time. It is also an inspiring account of a heroic life
dedicated to helping all people free themselves from suffering and
futility and attain true peace of mind.
(Middleway Press, paperback: ISBN 978-0-9779245-2-3; $14.95)

Buddhism, The First Millennium
By DAISAKU IKEDA
The second in the three-volume Soka Gakkai History
of Buddhism series

A major effort to formulate the Buddhist canon took place not long after the death of Shakyamuni Buddha at what is known as the First Council. Subsequently there arose differences of interpretation and a schism between the monastic community and the lay community. Nevertheless, Buddhism survived and developed. It came into contact with the West and spread eventually into Southeast Asia, China, Korea, and Japan. Contributing to this process were certain individuals—exceptional rulers like the Indian king Ashoka and the Greek philosopher-king Menander, in addition to monks and lay believers, including Vimalakirti, Nagarjuna, and Vasubandhu. Buddhism, The First Millennium portrays the coming of age of what is today a major world religion.
(Middleway Press, paperback: ISBN 978-0-9779245-3-0; $14.95)

FROM WORLD TRIBUNE PRESS

These titles can be purchased at SGI-USA bookstores nationwide or through the mail order center (call 800-626-1313 or e-mail mailorder@sgi-usa.org):

Kaneko's Story: A Conversation with Kaneko Ikeda
Kaneko Ikeda shares thoughts and stories of her youth, marriage and family and of supporting her husband of more than fifty-five years, SGI President Daisaku Ikeda. Also included are four messages written to the women of the SGI-USA.
(World Tribune Press, mail order #234302; $9.95)

My Dear Friends in America
BY DAISAKU IKEDA
This volume brings together for the first time all of the SGI president's speeches to U.S. members in the 1990s.
(World Tribune Press, paperback: SKU #204891; $15.95)

The New Human Revolution
BY DAISAKU IKEDA
An ongoing novelized history of the Soka Gakkai, which contains episodes from the past as well as guidance in faith that we can apply today.
(World Tribune Press; $12.00 each volume)

Volume 1, mail order #4601
Volume 2, mail order #4602
Volume 3, mail order #4603
Volume 4, mail order #4604
Volume 5, mail order #4605
Volume 6, mail order #4606
Volume 7, mail order #4607
Volume 8, mail order #4608
Volume 9, mail order #4609
Volume 10, mail order #4610
Volume 11, mail order #4611
Volume 12, mail order #4612
Volume 13, mail order #4613
Volume 14, mail order #4614
Volume 15, mail order #275446
Volume 16, SKU #275447
Volume 17, SKU #275448